S2F Tracke

in action

By Jim Sullivan

Color by Don Greer

Illustrated by Perry Manley & Joe Sewell

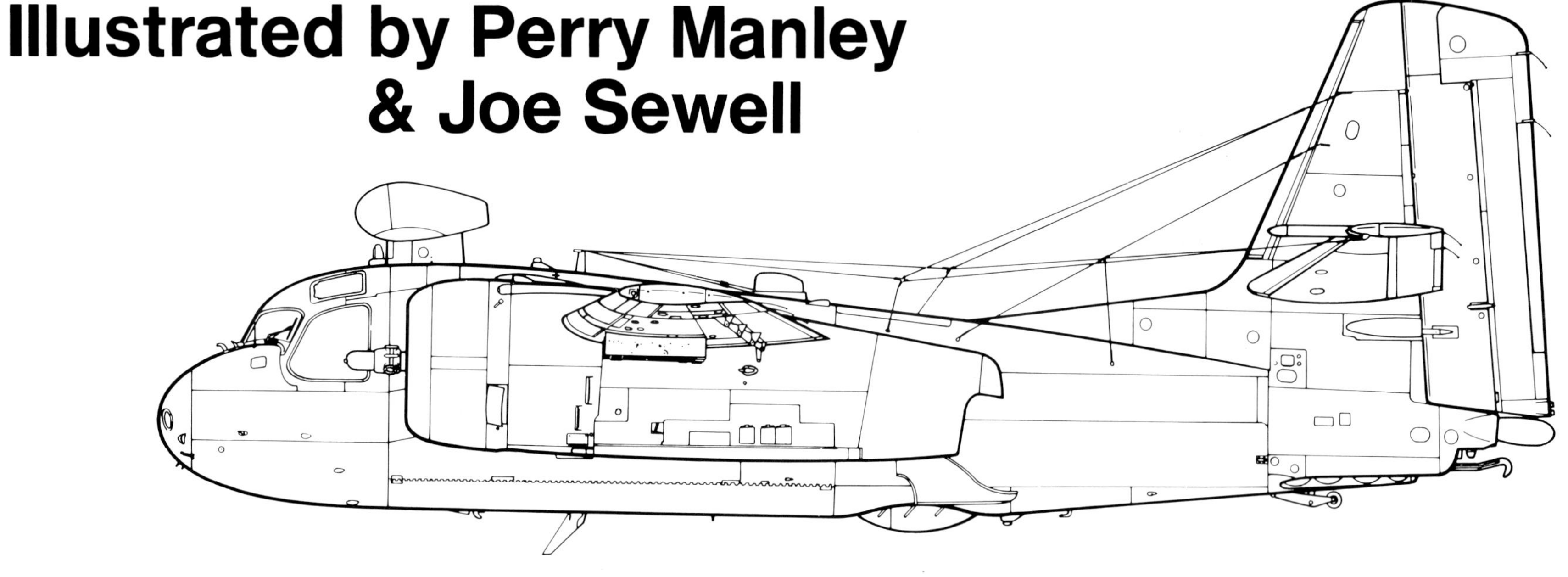

Aircraft Number 100

squadron/signal publications

An S-2E Tracker (NV-212/BuNo 151685) of VS-37, assigned to Carrier Anti-submarine Group 5, over the Pacific near San Diego, California, on 25 June 1969. VS-37 was home based at NAS North Island, Coronado, California.

ISBN 0-89747-242-X

If you have any photographs of the aircraft, armor, soldiers or ships of any nation, particularly wartime snapshots, why not share them with us and help make Squadron/Signal's books all the more interesting and complete in the future. Any photograph sent to us will be copied and the original returned. The donor will be fully credited for any photos used. Please send them to:

Squadron/Signal Publications, Inc.
1115 Crowley Drive.
Carrollton, TX 75011-5010.

Dedication

This book is dedicated to the pilots, aircrews and ground crews that flew and maintained the Grumman S2F Tracker/C-1 Trader/E-1 Tracer. Their combined efforts provided fleet ASW, coastal protection and Carrier Onboard Delivery (COD) services for nearly three decades. I would also like to dedicate this book to my wife, Linda, my son, Jim Jr., and my daughter, Christy. Each, in his or her own way, helped with the completion of this book.

Acknowledgements

I wish to thank all my contributors for their assistance with information and material for this book. Special appreciation must go to the following: Alan Weber, Albert Weber, Bud O'Toole, Bob Kowalski, Terry Panopalis, and Lois Lovisolo of Grumman Corporation. My sincere thanks to all:

Hal Andrews
Roger Besercker
Warren Bodie
Pete Bowers
Jim Burridge
Bill Curry
Robert F. Dorr
Carlton Eddy
Bob Esposito
Grumman Corporation
M. Herben
Clay Jansson
Bob Kowalski
W.T. Larkins
Bob Lawson/The Hook
Pat Leddy
Don Linn
Lois Lovisolo
Dave Lucabaugh
Marsh Aviation
Peter Mersky
Joe Michaels/JEM Aviation Slides
Paul McDaniel
Sam Morgan
Hediki Nagakubo
Sean C. Onken
Bud O'Toole
Terry Panopalis
Lionel Paul
Peter Russell-Smith
Bill Sides
Larry Smalley
U.S. Navy
Alan Weber
Albert Weber

An S2F-1S1 (S-2F/BuNo 136689) of VS-24 aboard USS INTREPID, piloted by LT Bud O'Toole, flies over a surfaced Russian WHISKEY class submarine in the Mediterranean Sea on 2 July 1964. (U.S. Navy via Bud O'Toole)

AU
136689
NAVY
VS-24
10
USS INTREPID

Introduction

The Second World War had demonstrated the tremendous destructive power of unrestricted submarine warfare and the need for specialized aircraft to combat this threat to the safe movement of men and supplies to the war fronts. The U.S. Navy successfully fought the U-Boat war and emerged from World War II with the most powerful Naval Air Force in the world. During the late 1940s and early 1950s, U.S. Naval strategy on Anti-Submarine Warfare (ASW) centered around the Hunter-Killer aircraft concept. Acting as a team, the Hunter aircraft would locate the target and the Killer aircraft would destroy it. The first aircraft types used for this mission were the TBM-3W (Hunter) and TBM-3S (Killer); both of which were derived from the Grumman Avenger torpedo bomber.

During the 1950s, the Avenger ASW team was replaced by the Grumman-built AF Guardian the largest, single engine aircraft to serve in the U.S. Navy. The Guardian was also used in the Hunter-Killer concept utilizing two variants, the AF-2W (Hunter) and AF-2S (Killer). Both the Avenger and Guardian required two aircraft acting as a team, which could have led to a problem if either aircraft developed mechanical problems. If that occurred, the mission could not be flown. In addition, both were single engine aircraft and the Navy wanted the reliability and safety that a twin engined aircraft would provide. With the solution to those two problems in mind, Grumman began work on a new ASW aircraft with two engines and with sufficient internal space for both sensors and armament in a single airframe.

The new ASW aircraft was first conceived during 1949 as the Grumman model G-89. Grumman submitted the design proposal to the U.S. Navy during early 1950. Its major advantage to the ASW mission was in combining both the Hunter and Killer roles into one aircraft, the G-89, which could handle both the detection and attack roles. The Navy ASW mission description consisted of: detecting, tracking and destroying enemy submarines; providing all-weather anti-submarine protection for convoy and Naval Task Forces; providing ASW barrier patrols for fixed geographical areas; locating enemy surface targets; conducting air reconnaissance operations; and, if needed, obtaining photographic records of all attacks and their results. The G-89 was the first ASW platform to combine all of these functions within a single airframe.

In June of 1950, the U.S. Navy gave Grumman the go-ahead to produce two prototypes of the G-89 under the designation XS2F-1 (BuNos 129137 and 129138). The first prototype emerged as a twin engined, high wing monoplane with tricycle landing gear and single wheel tail bumper installation. The aircraft featured a retractable belly-mounted radome and a tail mounted retractable Magnetic Anomaly Detection (MAD) boom. The XS2F-1 prototype carried a crew of four; pilot, co-pilot and two ASW systems operators. Provisions were made to carry two anti-submarine torpedoes in the fuselage weapons bay and three stations were provided under each wing for rockets or other ordnance. The aircraft was configured with catapult gear and an arresting hook to enable it to operate from carrier decks.

Powered by a pair of 1,500 hp Wright R-1820 Cyclone engines driving square tipped, three blade Hamilton Standard propellers, the first XS2F-1 prototype (BuNo 129137) flew on 4 December 1952. During February of 1953, the prototype began its initial flight evaluations at the Naval Air Test Center (NATC) Patuxent River, Maryland. By October of 1953, the second XS2F-1 (BuNo 129138) had joined the testing and this aircraft was used to conduct carrier suitability trials at Patuxent (Pax) River. The favorable results of

The first XS2F-1 (BuNo 129137) carries a test instrumentation probe on the starboard wing and a full load of six 5 inch HVAR rockets on the underwing pylons. (Grumman via Pete Bowers)

these trials and the tests at Pax River convinced the Navy to place an initial order for fifteen aircraft (BuNos 129139-129153) under the designation S2F-1.

Former Navy pilot Bob Kowalski, whose military flying career included both the Grumman-built AF Guardian and the S2F-1/S2F-2, compared the qualities of the two different aircraft:

> *In October of 1954, when VS-30 transitioned from the Grumman AF Guardian to the S2F, the change was not looked forward to by many pilots — we preferred the "greenhouse" spaciousness of the AF to the cramped closeness of the Tracker's two-man cockpit. Flying the S2F required a reversal of the hand roles. When flying the Guardian, the left hand would be on the throttle and the right hand on the joystick; the Tracker required the left hand on the control yoke and the right hand on the engine throttles which were mounted on the overhead panel. The benefits of the Tracker were apparent when the pilot strapped in and started the engines — the vastly improved forward visibility was most welcome. Gone also was the need to "S" turn while taxiing. Since direct forward visibility was non-existent in a "tail-dragger" like the AF Guardian, "S" turns were required to view the runway directly ahead while the plane was in a 3-point attitude. The S2F sat in a flight attitude on its tricycle gear and this gave the desired improvement in forward visibility. While taxiing the S2F, the lack of a steerable nosewheel was compensated for by the use of differential engine power and rudder pressure for runway turns. All things considered, the S2F was a great improvement over the AF Guardian.*

An AF-2W (SW-13) Guardian of VS-801 peels off, to be followed moments later by an AF-2S (SW-4) on 20 October 1952. This Hunter-Killer team served as the Fleet Anti-Submarine Warfare (ASW) aircraft from the late 1940s until 1954 when the S2F Tracker replaced them. (U.S. Navy)

An early production S2F-1 of VS-26 flies in formation with the Hunter-Killer aircraft it is replacing, a TBM-3W (SH-18/Hunter) and a TBM-3S (SH-1/Killer) during 1954. With the arrival of the S2F-1 Tracker, the Hunter and Killer functions were combined in one aircraft, eliminating the need for two aircraft Hunter-Killer teams. (U.S. Navy via Hal Andrews)

Development

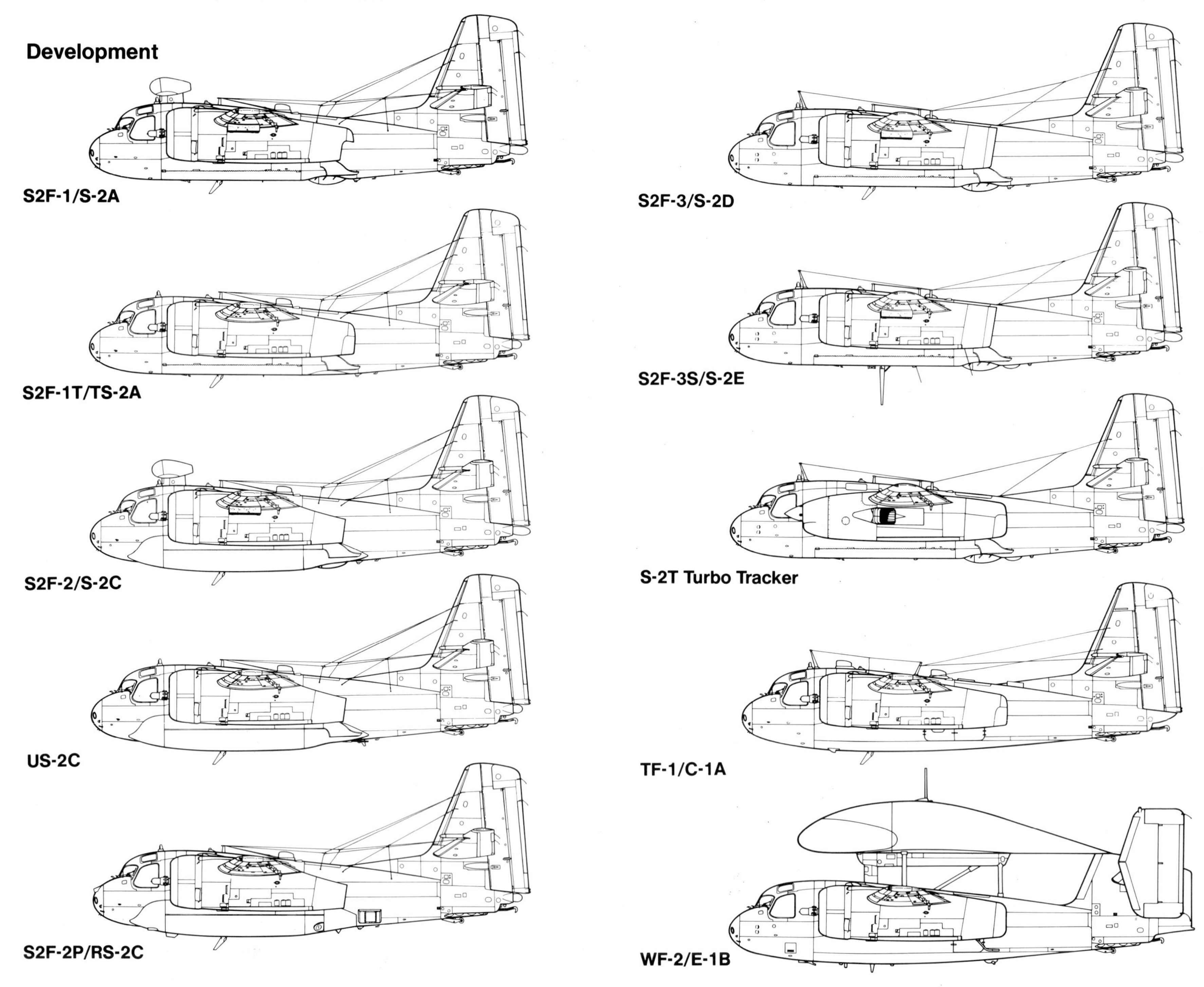

S2F-1 (S-2A)

Little change occurred between the prototype XS2F-1s and the production S2F-1. Production S2F-1s featured an uprated 1,525 hp Wright R-1820-82 engine in place of the 1,500 hp R-1820s used on the prototype. When Grumman first flew the production S2F-1 on 7 July 19 53 (BuNo 129139), the aircraft had not received its official name. For a brief time just after its introduction, the name Sentinel was used; however, this did not last long since the name was already in use by the Stinson L-5. The Navy finally officially named the S2F-1 the Tracker; although, unofficially the aircrews had adopted the name STOOF (S-TWO-F). Both names were heard throughout the Tracker's twenty-three year operational career. Late in 1962, when the Navy Department issued a sweeping redesignation of most of its aircraft, the S2F-1 was redesignated the S-2A.

Grumman, working closely with U.S. Navy requirements, installed the most modern ASW detection equipment available to hunt enemy submarines. With this sensor suite, the Tracker was capable of detecting, identifying and tracking submarines in all kinds of weather. With its internal armament, the Tracker could also attack and destroy the target. With the service introduction of the Tracker, the days of the two-aircraft Hunter-Killer concept were over.

With a full fuel load of 520 gallons of aviation gas, the S2F-1 had a combat range of 841 nautical miles and a flight endurance of just over six hours. Cruising speed of the Tracker was 130 knots (150 mph) with a top speed of 230 knots (265 mph). This performance was ideal for the long search missions and barrier patrols expected of a fleet ASW aircraft.

For hunting submarines, the Tracker was equipped with a belly-mounted radome containing an AN/APS 38 search radar. The radome was aerodynamically contoured and in the retracted position, fitting snugly within the fuselage, came within six inches of being completely flush with the fuselage undersurface. For ASW missions, the radome was lowered 24.5 inches to its fully extended position. The tail mounted retractable MAD boom could be extended nine feet behind the Tracker. Installed over the cockpit in early Trackers (up to BuNo 133239), was a bi-pole APA-69 ECM direction finding antenna. This installation was replaced by the AN/APA-69 radome mounted antenna on S2F-1 BuNo 133240 and subsequent S2F-1 Trackers. Both of these antennas were used for direction finding by the intercept of passive electronic emissions from submarine contacts. For identifying targets at night, early S2F-1s carried a powerful seventy million candlepower searchlight installed in a pod on the starboard wing. Later production S2F-1s and export variants provided to our allies under the MDAP (Mutual Defense Aid Program), were equipped with a more powerful eighty-five million candlepower searchlight.

Armament for the S2F-1 was carried on six underwing racks (three per wing) and/or in the internal weapons bay. Depending on the mission, the internal bay could house a Mk 34 or 43 ASW torpedo, bombs or depth charges. The underwing stations could carry 350 pounds on the inboard and outboard pylons and 265 pounds on the center pylons. Normal weapons carried on these pylons consisted of 5 inch HVAR rockets, bombs, Mk 54 depth charges, or 2.75 inch rocket pods.

The Tracker's wings had a unique folding arrangement. The hinge line was angled in such a way that the starboard wing folded slightly forward and the port wing, slightly aft. This arrangement kept the lowest profile possible for folded wing storage aboard carriers. For maximum lift efficiency, all Tracker variants (Trader and Tracer included) used a fixed wing slot on the undersurface of the outer wing panels just to the rear of the wing leading edge.

Each of the two engine nacelles were designed to carry eight SSQ-2 sonobuoys and a pair of larger SSQ-1 sonobouys (two top tubes) in drop tubes mounted at the extreme end

The 13th production S2F-1 (BuNo 129151) Tracker during its acceptance flight over Long Island, near Grumman's Bethpage factory. The bi-pole ECM direction finder antenna is mounted over and just to the rear of the cockpit. The overall Glossy Sea Blue paint scheme remained the standard factory applied finish until 1957. (Grumman via Pete Bowers)

This S2F-1 (BuNo 133237) has its Radome and Magnetic Anomaly Detector (MAD) boom fully extended as it would be during an ASW mission. The forward-raked mast on the fuselage underside and just forward of the weapons bay, is the barricade guard. (Grumman via Pete Bowers)

An S2F-1 (BuNo 133262) of VS-31 shares the ramp with a KC-97, F-89 and F-94C at New York during 1958. The S2F is Glossy Sea Blue with White codes and markings and was delivered with the APA-69 radome in place of the earlier bi-pole antenna installation. (F.G. Freeman via Bill Larkins)

This YS2F-1 (BuNo 129145) Tracker, with the uprated R1820-82 engines, was assigned to the Electronics Test (ET) section at the Naval Air Test Center (NATC), Patuxent River, Maryland, during December of 1967. (Ed Deigan via Pete Bowers)

of the nacelles. When released, these three foot long receiver/transmitter devices went into the sea where they picked up underwater noises made by a passing submarine and transmitted that data back to the Tracker, where the submarine's position was plotted. In addition to the sonobuoys, the rear of each nacelle also carried fifteen SUS (signal-underwater-sound) devices used for submarine location. The SUS device produced a small explosion which sent out sound waves in all directions. These would bounce off the submarine's hull and the direction and time of the return echo could be plotted, giving the exact location of the submarine. Late in the production run, the rear of the engine nacelle was modified with an aerodynamic fairing to improve airflow over the sonobuoy launchers. The profile of the modified nacelle quickly earned it the nickname, "Hawkbill."

With the MAD boom extended, The S2F-1 could measure the change in the earth's magnetic field induced by a submarine's metal hull. With the submarine's position plotted, the Tracker would drop a marine marker (white smoke) to visually mark the location. At that point, a run would be made to drop ordnance, either bombs, rockets, depth charges or torpedoes. With the Tracker's sophisticated ASW equipment and armament, the S2F-1 was a deadly threat to enemy submarines.

The S2F-1 Tracker joined the Fleet during 1954 and first went to sea aboard USS PRINCETON with Anti-Submarine Squadron (VS) 23 for a WESTPAC deployment.

Several variants evolved from the S2F-1, including the US-2A, S2F-1T (TS-2A), S2F-1S (S-2B/US-2B) and the S2F-1S1 (S-2F). By the time the final S2F-1 had rolled off the assembly line, a total of 755 aircraft had been built. 625 of these were intended for the U.S. Navy and 130 were built for export under MDAP. In addition to the Grumman-built Trackers, deHavilland of Canada produced 99 aircraft under license as CS2F-1/CS2F-2 aircraft.

Commenting on the S2F-1 Tracker, former Naval Aviator, Bob Kowalski remembers:

...on the runway and cleared for takeoff, the throttles were advanced to 54 inches of Mercury and the Tracker would accelerate quickly (compared to Bob's former aircraft, the

S2F-1 Number 10 of VS-30 makes a three-point carrier approach during Field Carrier Landing Practice (FCLP) at NAALF Fentress near Virginia Beach, Virginia, during February of 1955. The LSO has already given the pilot the signal to land. (Bob Kowalski)

SL-15, an S2F-1 (BuNo 133277) of VS-22, is parked with folded wings on the ramp at Boston. This tracker was stationed at NAS Key West, Florida, during November of 1954 and had the rudder and fin tip trimmed in White. (U.S. Navy via Hal Andrews)

This S2F-1, flown by ENS William Y. Sneed of VS-21, completes the 59,000th landing aboard USS PRINCETON on 21 October 1955. VS-21's unit marking was a Red lightning bolt on a White field and was carried on the outside of both engine nacelles and on the tip of the fin. (U.S. Navy via Hal Andrews)

This S2F-1 (BuNo 136412) of VS-20 flew from USS PRINCETON to NAS Ford Island, Hawaii, during 1956. The aircraft carries small practice depth charges on the six underwing racks. The unit markings on the tail are Intermediate Blue with four White stars. (Al Weber via Alan Weber)

AF Guardian)...at about 50 knots the rudder response became effective and at about 95 knots, the S2F-1 seemed to 'leap' into the air. Once airborne in the Tracker and as the landing gear retracted, a nose-up pitch movement occurred. This was usually controlled by a nose-down trim change to help the pilot maintain a constant climb out attitude. The S2F-1 handled well in flight and was quite an improvement over the earlier AF Guardian.

Looking at the complete Tracker line, the S2F (S-2) served the Navy for 23 years, flew over 6,100,000 hours (about 1 billion miles), made over 744,400 carrier landings on over forty U.S. and foreign aircraft carriers and served in the armed forces of fourteen foreign countries.

ECM Direction Finder Antenna

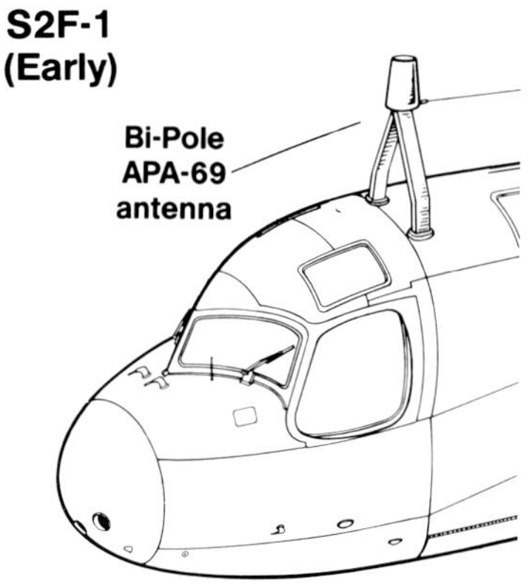

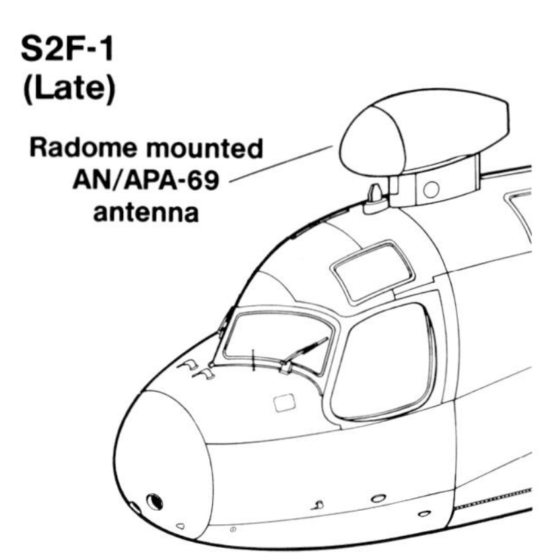

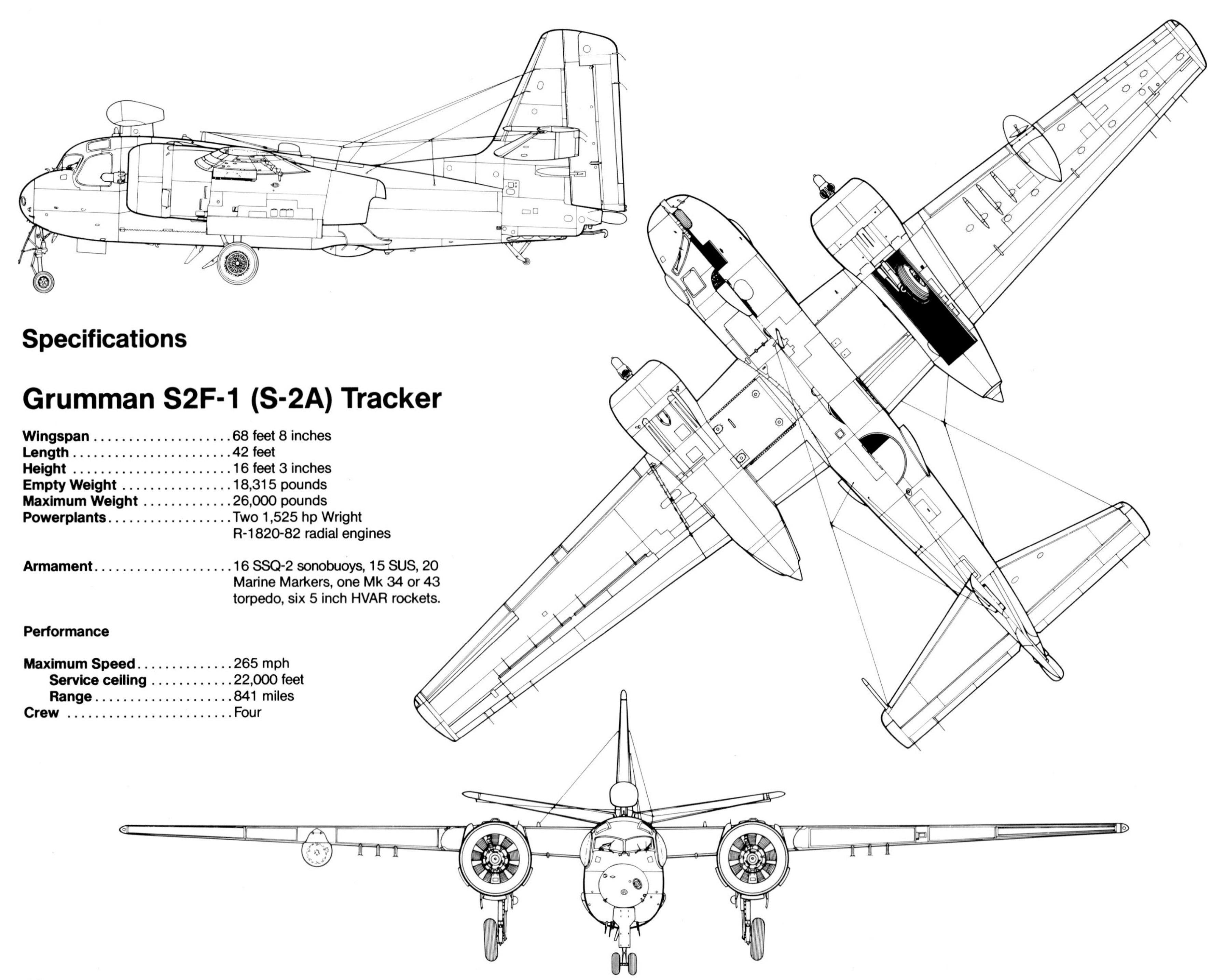

Specifications

Grumman S2F-1 (S-2A) Tracker

Wingspan .... 68 feet 8 inches
Length .... 42 feet
Height .... 16 feet 3 inches
Empty Weight .... 18,315 pounds
Maximum Weight .... 26,000 pounds
Powerplants .... Two 1,525 hp Wright R-1820-82 radial engines

Armament .... 16 SSQ-2 sonobuoys, 15 SUS, 20 Marine Markers, one Mk 34 or 43 torpedo, six 5 inch HVAR rockets.

Performance

Maximum Speed .... 265 mph
Service ceiling .... 22,000 feet
Range .... 841 miles
Crew .... Four

An overall Glossy Sea Blue S2F-1 (133047) of VS-26 on patrol over the Atlantic. The aircraft carried White lettering and a borderless national insignia. VS-26 was based at NAS Norfolk, Virginia, during 1955. (U.S. Navy via Pete Bowers)

This S2F-1 (BuNo 133103) on the ramp at NAS Oakland, California, on 16 September 1956, carries an International Orange fuselage band indicating that it was assigned to the Naval Reserves. The pilot's escape hatch on top of the fuselage is in the open position. (Bill Larkins)

S2F-1s of VS-27 line up for deck launch aboard USS WASP as she steams off the Virginia coast. During 1957 the Navy changed the tactical paint scheme carried on carrier aircraft and it was not uncommon to see aircraft within the same squadron in both the Glossy Sea Blue finish and the new Gull Gray over White scheme. (U.S. Navy via Hal Andrews)

S2F-1s of VS-22 wait at the end of the runway at NAS Key West, Florida, during March of 1956 as ordnance crews arm their weapons. The lead Tracker carried the squadron insignia on the fuselage just below the cockpit. (U.S. Navy via Hal Andrews)

This S2F-1 (BuNo 133131) assigned to the Pacific Missile Range at Point Mugu, California, carries a streamlined loudspeaker pod on the port outer wing pylon on 22 April 1961. The pod consisted of four large speakers, with a nose and tail fairing. The pod was used to warn boaters to clear the test range prior to a missile launch. (Clay Jansson)

This S2F-1 (BuNo 136482) of VS-36 is loaded with inert 5-inch HVAR rockets and depth charges on the underwing pylons for a display during 1960. The lines coming off the trailing edges of the wing and horizontal stabilizer are static electricity dischargers. (Pete Bowers Collection)

An S-2A (S2F-1/BuNo 136400) of VS-35 makes a practice low level delivery of an aerial torpedo from its weapons bay during 1963. The primary torpedo carried was the Mk 43 ASW acoustic homing torpedo. (U.S. Navy via Peter Mersky collection)

Engine Nacelle

S2F-1 (Early)

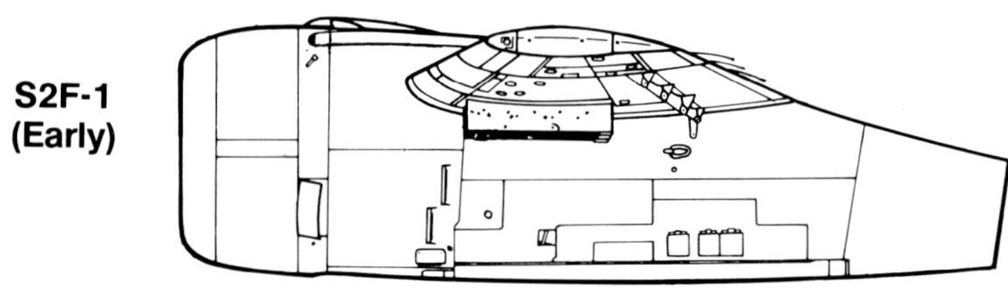

S2F-1 (Late)

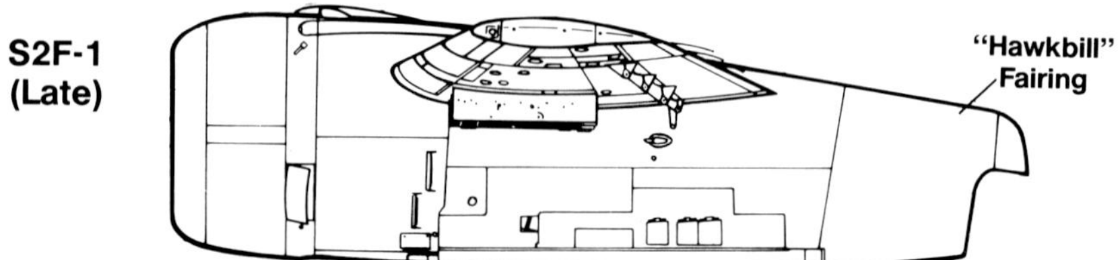

A pair of S2F-1 Trackers of VS-31 are parked on the deck of USS WASP during the Winter of 1959. The Tracker had an unusual wing fold system; the starboard wing folded in front of the port wing. (Grumman)

An S2F-1 (136432) of VS-23, in its newly painted Gull Gray over White scheme, is parked on display at Salinas, California, on 22 September 1957. The squadron insignia under the cockpit is a Black Panther holding a submarine in its jaws. (Larry Smalley)

An S-2A (S2F-1/BuNo 136701) of VS-21 flies an ASW search mission with the belly radome and MAD boom deployed. NS-15 was operating off the coast of San Diego, California, on 18 December 1963 and carried a Red lighting bolt, outlined in Black, on the rudder and a Red fin tip. (U.S. Navy)

An S2F-1 (BuNo 136571) of VS-36 is hoisted aboard USS RANDOLPH (CVS-15) during November of 1959. At the time RANDOLPH was a dedicated ASW carrier and carried a mix of S2Fs and HSS-1 (H-34) ASW helicopters. (U.S. Navy via Peter Mersky collection)

US-2A

To provide the Navy with a multi-engine utility aircraft to replace the aging C-45 and other utility aircraft then in use, fifty-one S2F-1 Trackers were converted to the limited utility role under the designation US-2A. The conversion consisted of the removal of all internal ASW equipment, the belly-mounted radome, the MAD boom, the AN/APA-69 antenna radome over the cockpit and the wing-mounted searchlight. Although not actually removed, the nacelle mounted sonobuoy launchers were faired over with a tapered, streamlined fairing. All gear pertaining to carrier operations was retained and the US-2A continued to use the dependable R-1820-82 engines with square-tipped, three blade Hamilton Standard propellers.

The US-2A was considerably lighter than a standard S-2A and, besides it normal utility mission, could be equipped as a target-towing aircraft for Fleet gunnery practice, both surface and aerial. The US-2A Tracker was also capable of carrying light cargo loads and was very useful for delivering high priority supplies to carriers at sea. A number of the US-2As also entered service with the U.S. Marine Corps and were used primarily for multi-engine proficiency flying by senior station pilots.

This US-2A (BuNo 133317) of VX-4 at NAS Point Magu, California, on 7 July 1972, carries the "double-nuts" side number 100 reserved for the squadron commander. The two zeros in the nose number are in the shape of octagonal nuts. The unit markings are White stars on a Dark Blue field and were carried on the nacelles, wingtips and top of the fin. (Peter Mancus)

Based at MCAS Futema, Japan, this US-2A (BuNo 136613) was on final approach to NAF Atsugi, Japan, during May of 1971. When serving outside the United States, an American flag was usually painted on the aircraft high on the vertical fin. (Hediki Nagakubo)

Utility Conversion

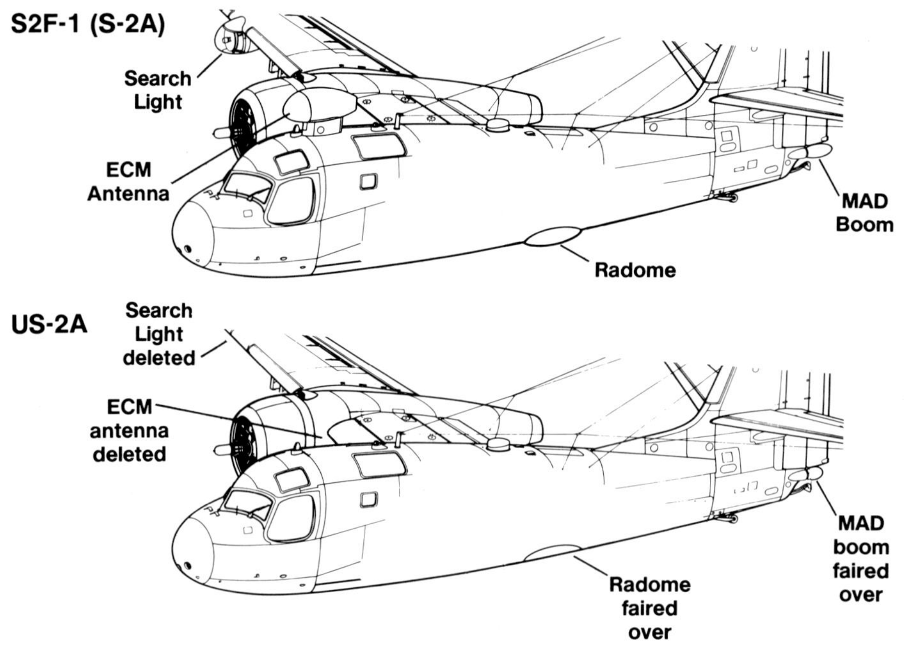

On final approach to the duty runway, a US-2A (BuNo 133317) from MCAF New River, North Carolina, lands at Shaw AFB, South Carolina, on 18 June 1970. The US-2A had all ASW equipment deleted and target tow capability added. (Jim Sullivan)

A US-2A (BuNo 136529) assigned to the Naval Air Facility at Washington, DC, on 24 April 1973 begins folding its wing after departing the duty runway on its way to its assigned spot on the ramp. (Jim Sullivan)

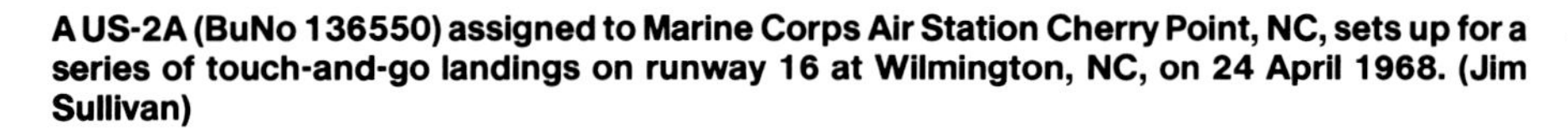

A US-2A (BuNo 136550) assigned to Marine Corps Air Station Cherry Point, NC, sets up for a series of touch-and-go landings on runway 16 at Wilmington, NC, on 24 April 1968. (Jim Sullivan)

S2F-1T (TS-2A)

To provide the Navy with both an ASW trainer and a multi-engine trainer that closely approximated the characteristics of current fleet multi-engine aircraft, approximately 200 S2F-1 airframes were converted as trainers under the designation S2F-1T (TS-2A).

With the introduction of the S2F-1T (TS-2A), the training of future multi-engine qualified Naval Aviators was now handled by the Tracker. TS-2As assigned to Training Command as multi-engine trainers were modified with all ASW gear being deleted, including the radomes, MAD boom and wing-mounted searchlight.

Aircraft intended as ASW crew trainers retained their ASW gear and simply had the designation changed from S2F-1 to S2F-1T. These aircraft normally carried up to twenty-five Mk 15 Mod 8 practice depth charges internally in place of their normal armaments, the wing stations were used for practice rockets and bombs.

In the training role, pilots selected for multi-engine training received 140 flight hours in the TS-2A, flying day and night familiarization, basic instrument, day and night navigation, ASW tactics and carrier qualifications on a fleet carrier. This training was ultimately carried out by three training squadrons; VT-27, VT-28 and VT-31, all based at NAS Corpus Christi, Texas. Eventually, the TS-2A Trainer was replaced in the Navy Training Command by the Beech T-44.

A TS-2A (S2F-1T/BuNo 133204) of VT-28 rumbles down the taxiway at NAS Corpus Christi, Texas, on 30 April 1974. The TS-2A was used to train student multi-engine pilots at this key training base. (U.S. Navy via Peter Mersky Collection)

An S2F-1T (TS-2A/BuNo 133148) of VT-27 launches from the angled deck of USS ANTIETAM on 13 February 1958. High-visibility Red/Orange trainer markings were carried over an overall White paint scheme. (U.S. Navy via Hal Andrews)

This TS-2A (BuNo 136497) of VT-31 on the ramp at NAS Lemoore, California, on 10 May 1970, carried colorful Red unit markings in a scheme unique to that squadron. The aircraft was overall White with Black lettering. (Clay Jansson)

This S2F-1T (BuNo 133179) of Advanced Training Unit (ATU) 611 carried the colorful White and Red/Orange markings used to identify trainer aircraft. The squadron was later redesignated VT-28, and was one of three training squadrons based at NAS Corpus Christi, Texas, during 1960. (Pete Bowers Collection)

A student pilot and his instructor fly a TS-2A (S2F-1T/BuNo 136507) of VT-27 off the coast of Southwest Texas, on 20 June 1968. Trackers were used by the Training Command as advanced trainers to provide qualified multi-engine pilots for the fleet. (U.S. Navy via Hal Andrews)

This TS-2A (136530) of VT-31 begins folding its wings as it taxies to the parking deck area aboard a training carrier on 20 June 1968. The student pilots then changed seats and the Tracker "Trainer" was launched again. (U.S. Navy via Hal Andrews)

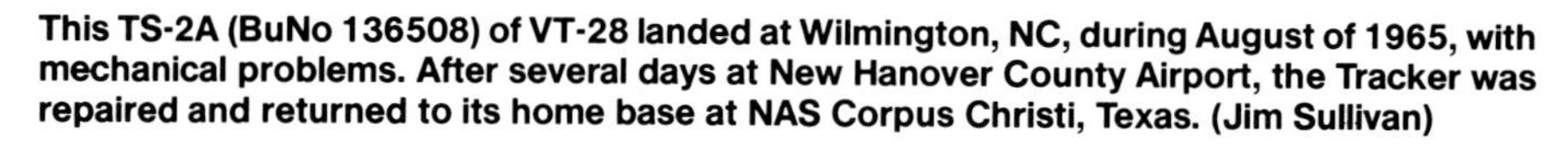
This TS-2A (BuNo 136508) of VT-28 landed at Wilmington, NC, during August of 1965, with mechanical problems. After several days at New Hanover County Airport, the Tracker was repaired and returned to its home base at NAS Corpus Christi, Texas. (Jim Sullivan)

US-2B

Like the earlier US-2A, the US-2B was a utility variant of the Tracker converted from S2F-1 (S-2A) airframes, with one exception; the US-2B had the added capability of carrying five passengers.

The conversion consisted of removal of all internal ASW equipment, fairing over the belly radome opening and the MAD boom opening, and removal of the wing mounted searchlight. The space formerly used by the ASW electronics was converted to a passenger compartment capable of holding five passenger seats. In addition to hauling passengers, the US-2B could also carry light cargo loads in the space formerly taken up by the weapons bay. Alternatively, the former weapons bay could also be used to house additional fuel cells to extend the range of the US-2B. As with the earlier US-2A, the US-2B had the engine nacelle ends faired over.

Approximately seventy-five S-2A Tracker airframes were modified to the US-2B configuration. These aircraft saw wide-spread service and after a career lasting over twenty years, the last US-2B (BuNo 136475) was retired at NAS Whiting Field, Florida, on 14 October 1982. Upon its official retirement, the aircraft was flown to Davis Monthan AFB, AZ, and placed in storage.

The nose cap on this US-2B (BuNo 133306), at NAF Washington, on 2 June 1967, is open and held in position by a brace on the starboard side. This particular Tracker retained its ASW gear, but carried the US-2B designation under the horizontal stabilizer. (Clay Jansson)

Colorful Red, White and Blue markings decorate this "Fightertown USA" (NAS Miramar, California) US-2B (BuNo 136546) on the ramp at Miramar on 16 November 1972. "Snoopy" with a machine gun was carried high on the vertical fin. (Clay Jansson)

A US-2B (BuNo 136433) from NAF Washington, DC, settles onto the duty runway at MCAS Cherry Point, NC, on 13 November 1970. The US-2B had the belly radome and rear engine nacelles faired over. (Jim Sullivan)

(Below) A US-2B (BuNo 136552) of AES-12 is parked by its hangar at MCAS Quantico, Virginia, on 15 May 1969. When parked, US-2s frequently had their wings folded to conserve space on the ramp. (Jim Sullivan)

S2F-1S (S-2B)

The S2F-1S (S-2B) designation was applied to a number of S-2A Trackers which were modernized with the installation of updated ASW electronic sensors. This modernization program included the installation of the JEZEBEL acoustic search system and the JULIE acoustic echo ranging system. As with the earlier S2F-1 Tracker, the 1,525 HP R-1820-82 powerplants were retained giving the S2F-1S a cruising speed of 130 knots (150 mph) at a gross weight of 26,000 pounds. The S-2B was an interim variant and saw limited service, flying only with the U.S. Navy. As more advanced versions of the Tracker entered service, the S-2B was rapidly phased out.

(Right) This S2F-1S (S-2B/BuNo 136610) of VS-33 is on display aboard the USS BENNINGTON (CVS-20) for an open house at NAS North Island, California, during August of 1960. (Clay Jansson)

(Below) An S2F-1S (S-2B/BuNo 136500) of VS-33 is chocked on the ramp at NAS Oakland, California, on 14 September 1962, with the nose towbar still attached to the nose gear strut. The propeller hub and fin tip are in Red. (Doug Olson via Clay Jansson)

S2F-1S1 (S-2F)

Externally identical to the S2F-1, the S2F-1S1 (S-2F) was an updated variant that saw widespread use with the U.S. Navy. The modernization program centered around the ASW electronics carried in the S2F and included the installation of an improved version of the JULIE acoustic echo ranging system. The S-2F served with fleet squadrons, the Reserves and a small number were exported under the Mutual Defense Assistance Program.

The S2F-1S1 was the final S2F-1 variant. Up to this time, all changes to the S2F had been internal, mainly in the electronic sensors installed, such as the updated JULIE equipment. Externally, the S2F-1S1 (S-2F) differed little from the XS2F-1 prototype.

Because it entered service after 1957 when the Navy changed its aircraft camouflage from Glossy Sea Blue to Gull Gray over Gloss White, the S-2F was delivered from the factory in the new camouflage scheme.

This S-2F (BuNo 136575) carries the 6S tail marking of a reserve unit assigned to NAS Norfolk, Virginia, during June of 1967. The S-2F Tracker was the final updated variant of the S2F-1 series. (U.S. Navy via Sam Morgan)

This S-2F (BuNo 136485) was assigned to the Pacific Missile Range as a range clearing aircraft and carried the range patch on the fin. The forward radome installation was used for surface search, scanning for small vessels in the missile test range. (Clay Jansson)

An S-2F (S2F-1S1/BuNo 136506) of VS-24 on final approach to a carrier landing on 20 November 1963, has its wheels, flaps, and tail hook down. VS-24 was stationed at NAS Norfolk, Virginia. (U.S. Navy via Bud O'Toole)

This S-2F (BuNo 144728) of VS-21 at NAS North Island on 2 May 1964, carries the markings of Carrier Anti-Submarine Group 53 (CVSG-53) in Black on the engine nacelle. The squadron insignia was carried on the fuselage sides beneath the cockpit on both sides. (Clay Jansson)

Canadian Trackers

During 1956, deHavilland of Canada acquired one Grumman S2F-1 Tracker for testing and evaluation. Upon selection as the Royal Canadian Navy's new ASW aircraft, deHavilland negotiated a license production agreement with Grumman and became the prime contractor for production of the S2F in Canada. Many Canadian companies shared in the manufacture of the Trackers, with sub-contractors being responsible for the wings, nacelles, landing gear and electronics. Final assembly was undertaken by deHavilland at their plant in Downsview, Canada.

The pattern Tracker (RCN 1501) was delivered to the Canadian Navy test and evaluation squadron, VX-10 during 1956 for a period of evaluation and trials. This aircraft was joined, during September of 1957, by an S2F-1 (BuNo 136519/RCN 1500) which was obtained from U.S. Navy stocks.

The first production CS2F-1 was accepted by the Royal Canadian Navy and was assigned to VS-881 on 7 February 1957. The squadron embarked in HMCS BONAVENTURE on 27 September 1957 for its first at sea deployment. In October of 1957 a second squadron, VS-880, was re-equipped with the Tracker. In Canadian Navy service, the Tracker originally served in the ASW role as it did with the U.S. Navy. In July of 1959 VS-881 was disbanded, leaving VS-880 as the sole ASW squadron, although two Utility Squadrons (VU) also operated the Tracker.

Under the terms of the license agreement between Grumman and deHavilland Aircraft of Canada, a total of 99 Trackers (in two variants) were produced by deHavilland. The first production variant was designated the CS2F-1 and was, externally, virtually identical to the Grumman-built S2F-1 differing mainly in the antennas carried on the aircraft. None of the Canadian-built Trackers carried the APA-69 ECM direction finder radome above the fuselage, most having a smaller square antenna in the same location. A total of forty-four CS2F-1s were produced.

As a result of proposed improvements suggested by the Royal Canadian Navy (RCN), deHavilland produced fifty-five updated Trackers under the designation CS2F-2. The improvements incorporated in the CS2F-2 were the addition of an improved MAD system, an uprated radar and improvements in ASW sensors. Externally there was little difference between the two models, except in antennas.

Between 1964 and 1967, a mid-life update was performed on the Canadian Trackers. The update consisted of the installation of the ASN-501 tactical computer/navigational system, APN-503 Doppler radar and improved JULIE/JEZEBEL ASW sensors. After updating, the Trackers were redesignated as CS2F-3s. It should be noted that the Canadian Trackers, despite their similar designations, were not equivalents of U.S. Navy S2F-1, S2F-2 or S2F-3 aircraft.

During 1964, two CS2F-1 Trackers were modified for the Carrier On Board Delivery (COD) role by deleting all ASW gear and installing six passenger seats, safety equipment and a fuel cell in the weapons bay. These aircraft were assigned to VU-32 in January of 1965 and flew from HMCS BONAVENTURE until the ship was retired from Canadian service in December of 1969.

In February of 1968, the Royal Canadian Navy, Royal Canadian Army and Royal Canadian Air Force were united, forming the Canadian Armed Forces. The Navy now became known as the Maritime Command. A tri-service designation system was also adopted and the Trackers were redesignated as CP-121s.

In December of 1973, the decision was made to delete all ASW equipment from the Trackers and utilize them in the maritime surveillance role. At this same time VS-880 was redesignated as Maritime Reconnaissance Squadron (MR) 880. During the late 1970s, the remaining Trackers in Canadian service were modified with updated search radar, navigational systems and communications equipment. More recently, the aircraft were further modified to carry photo reconnaissance pods on the wing pylons. Additionally, the aircraft are now configured to carry CRV-7 HVAR rocket pods and all have the capability of carrying SKAD (Survival Kit Air Dropable) pods on the wing pylons for Search and Rescue work.

Recently, one Tracker has been re-engined with turboprop engines under a program being developed by the IMP Group of Halifax, Nova Scotia (similar to the Turbo-Tracker developed by Marsh Aviation of Mesa, Arizona). At this time, there are eighteen Trackers remaining in service with MR-880, VU-33 and two reserve squadrons (Nos 406 and 420). Another eleven aircraft are also available, being currently held in storage. If recently announced plans for budget reductions go through, all CAF Trackers will be retired shortly, after thirty-two years of service.

Recently, the Brazilian Navy announced that it has placed a 40 million (Canadian) dollar contract with IMP for modification of its remaining eleven Trackers to the turboprop configuration for operation from the Brazilian carrier MINAS GERAIS. The re-engining program is expected to not only improve the aircraft's performance, it also ends a problem that the Brazilian Air Force has had with S-2 basing. Currently, the S-2s can only be operated from bases where AVGAS (aviation gasoline) is available, restricting its use in the maritime reconnaissance role. The first conversions are planned to be done in Canada, while others will be performed by Brazilian Air Force crews with kits supplied by IMP. The re-engine program is expected to extend the service life of the Brazilian S-2s well into the next century.

A number of other countries have also expressed interest in converting their Trackers to turboprop configurations, including South Korea and Taiwan.

The author wishes to acknowledge Terry Panopalis, for his valuable input on the history of Canadian Trackers.

A deHavilland of Canada produced CS2F-2 (RCN 1552), of the Royal Canadian Navy on the ramp at Philadelphia for a refueling stop during 1960. The RCN received their first Trackers during 1957. (Bob Esposito Collection)

A flight of CS2F-2 Trackers (1598/1573/1565/1596) of the Royal Canadian Navy. These Trackers were assigned to the Canadian aircraft carrier HMCS BONAVENTURE during 1966. (Terry Panopalis Collection)

This CS2F-3 (12187) of Maritime Reconnaissance Squadron 880 (MR-880) is roped off for a display on 29 June 1986. The aircraft carries a streamlined, day/night photographic pod on the outboard starboard wing pylon. The aircraft is used primarily for maritime reconnaissance, flying from CFB Shearwater, Nova Scotia. (Terry Panopalis)

Antenna Configuration

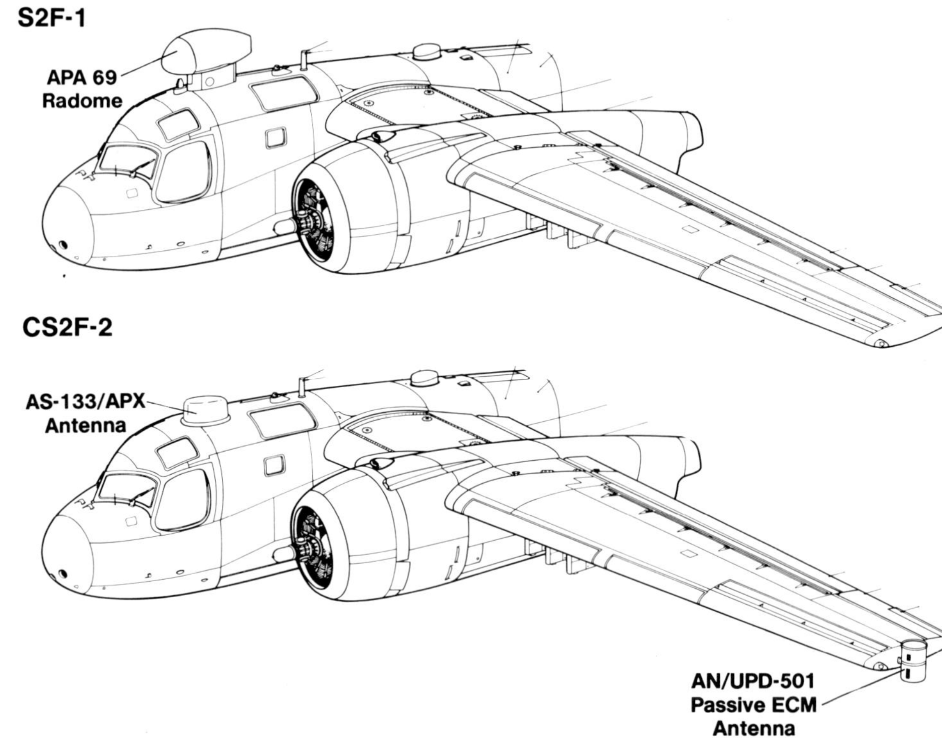

A CS2F-3 (12168) of MR-880 with the weapons bay open reveals the weapons bay auxiliary fuel tank installation used to extend the range of the Tracker for maritime reconnaissance missions. (Terry Panopalis)

Canadian Trackers are configured to carry six, six shot CRV-7 HVAR rocket launcher pods on the wing pylons. (Terry Panopalis)

A CAF CS2F-3 (12189) of VS-880 on the ramp at Pease AFB, NH, during an exchange visit in July of 1979. The squadron was home based at CFB Shearwater, Halifax, Nova Scotia. (Jim Burridge)

S2F-2 (S-2C)

The S2F-1 suffered from one major draw-back; its weapons bay was too small to handle the bulky early model nuclear depth charges in service during the 1950s. With this in mind, Grumman redesigned the S2F fuselage to accommodate a larger weapons bay. This redesign resulted in the S2F-2 (S-2C) and Grumman built sixty of this variant for the U.S. Navy (BuNo 133329-133388).

Externally the S2F-2 differed from the earlier S2F-1 in having an enlarged weapons bay fitted on the port underside of the fuselage. This resulted in a bulge to the port side of the S2F-2 fuselage (later reduction in the size of the nuclear depth charge enabled it to be carried by all Tracker variants). The wing stations of the S2F-2 were strengthened and cleared for carrying the Aero 6A rocket launcher pods.

To improve the aircraft's handling, especially at low speeds, the horizontal stabilizer was increased in span from 22 feet 4 inches to 27 feet 2 inches. The S2F-2 retained the same crew complement, powerplants, and internal ASW equipment as the earlier S2F-1. To test the aerodynamics of the new weapons bay, Grumman built a weapons bay mockup section which was installed on an S2F-1 airframe for flight tests.

The first production S2F-2 (S-2C/BuNo 133329) made its initial flight on 12 July 1954. One month later, the U.S. Navy conducted its preliminary aircraft evaluation, with the trials running from 11 through 14 August 1954. The fourth production S2F-2 (BuNo 133332) joined the test program and was used for carrier suitability trials conducted at NATC Patuxent River during early April of 1955. This Tracker was then embarked in USS BENNINGTON for shipboard carrier suitability demonstrations. The tests ran from 27 April to 4 May 1955, after which the S2F-2 was declared acceptable for shipboard operations. The first production S2F-2 (BuNo 133331) to be destined for squadron service was delivered to the Navy on 22 November 1954.

Former Naval Aviator Bob Kowalski remembers the S2F-2:

...when the S2F-2 was introduced, S2F-1 drivers incurred a big surprise! Grumman reversed the pitch trim mechanism so that the S2F-2 would not pitch-up on landing gear retraction as it did with the S2F-1. The 2nd Tracker model now pitched down. The word of this trait quickly spread among fleet pilots. As a result, the technique evolved to leave the landing gear in the down position until a safe altitude was attained.

As the S2F-2 (S-2C) was replaced by newer Tracker variants, a number were converted to the utility role under the designation of US-2C, Stripped of their ASW equipment, these aircraft were used primarily as target-tows.

This S2F-1 (BuNo 133063) served as the prototype for the S2F-2. It carried a mock-up of the enlarged weapons bay and was used for flight testing of the design. The standard S2F-1 tail was retained for the tests. (Grumman via Pete Bowers)

Weapons Bay/Engine Nacelle

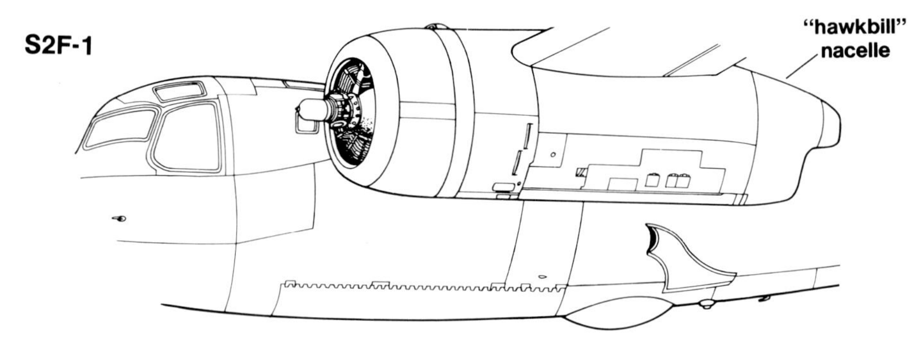

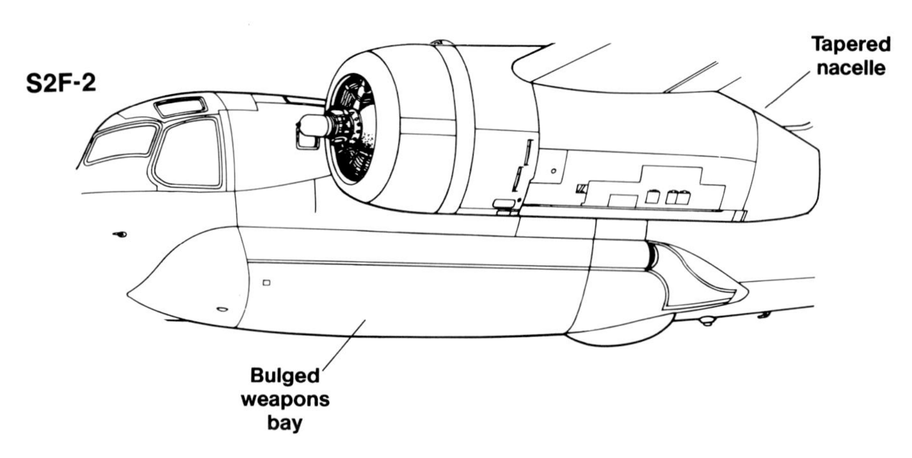

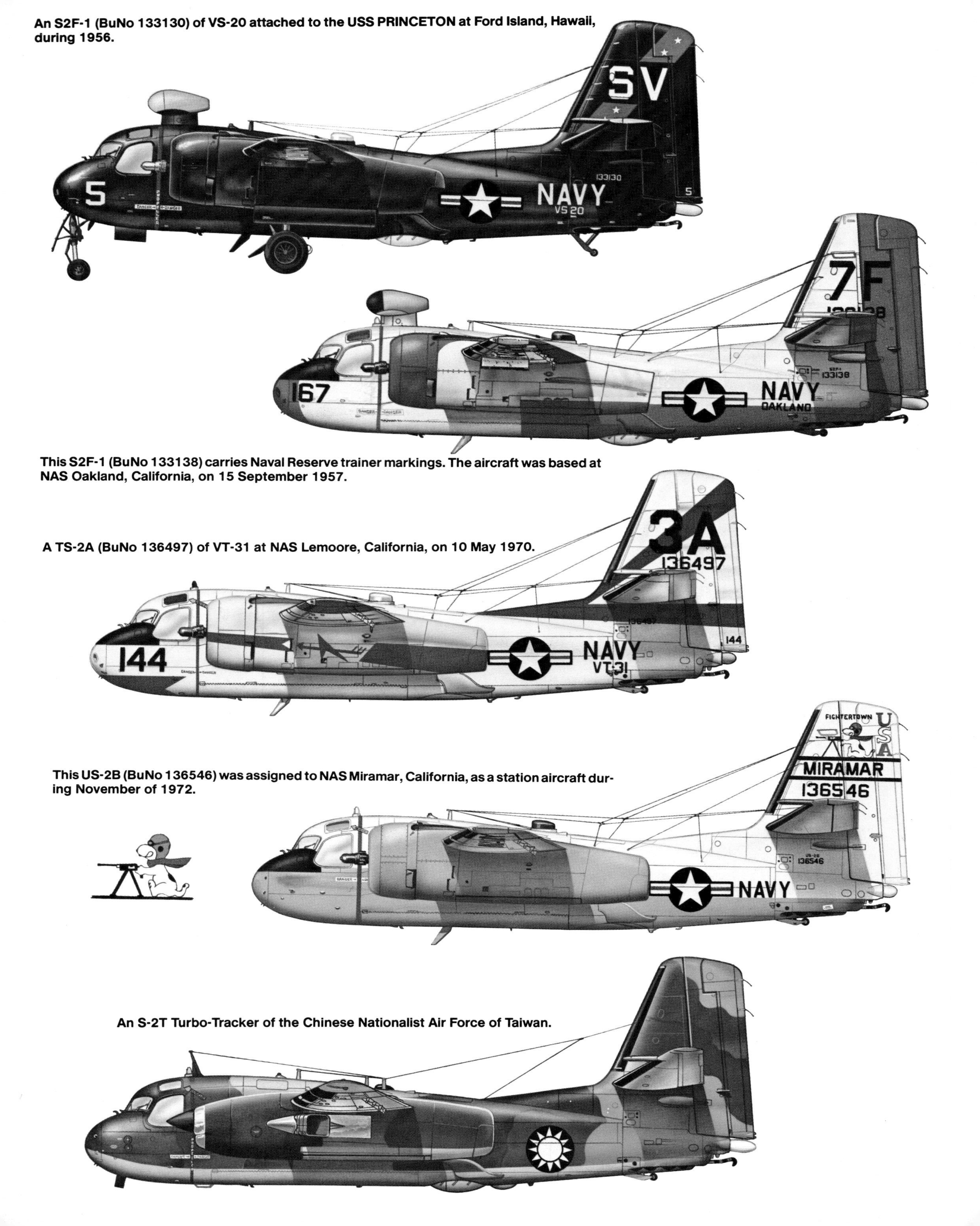

An S2F-1 (BuNo 133130) of VS-20 attached to the USS PRINCETON at Ford Island, Hawaii, during 1956.

This S2F-1 (BuNo 133138) carries Naval Reserve trainer markings. The aircraft was based at NAS Oakland, California, on 15 September 1957.

A TS-2A (BuNo 136497) of VT-31 at NAS Lemoore, California, on 10 May 1970.

This US-2B (BuNo 136546) was assigned to NAS Miramar, California, as a station aircraft during November of 1972.

An S-2T Turbo-Tracker of the Chinese Nationalist Air Force of Taiwan.

An S2F-2 (S-2C/BuNo 133385) of VS-21 at NAS Oakland, California, on 14 January 1959.

S2F-3 Tracker (S-2D/BuNo 149235) of VS-36 at Andrews AFB, Maryland, on 19 May 1965.

This S-2E (BuNo 153572) was assigned to VS-24 aboard the USS INTREPID during September of 1971.

VX-5 painted this C-1A (BuNo 136782) in very colorful Bicentennial markings during 1976.

This E-1B Tracer (BuNo 148132) of VAW-11 was assigned to USS HANCOCK during 1965.

An early production S2F-2 (BuNo 133330) during factory acceptance flights. The horizontal stabilizer of the S2F-2 was nearly five feet longer than the earlier S2F-1 and the weapons bay was enlarged to accommodate larger ordnance loads. (Grumman)

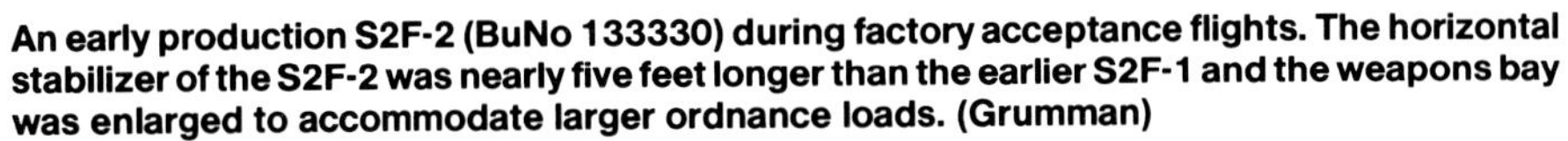

Horizontal Stabilizer

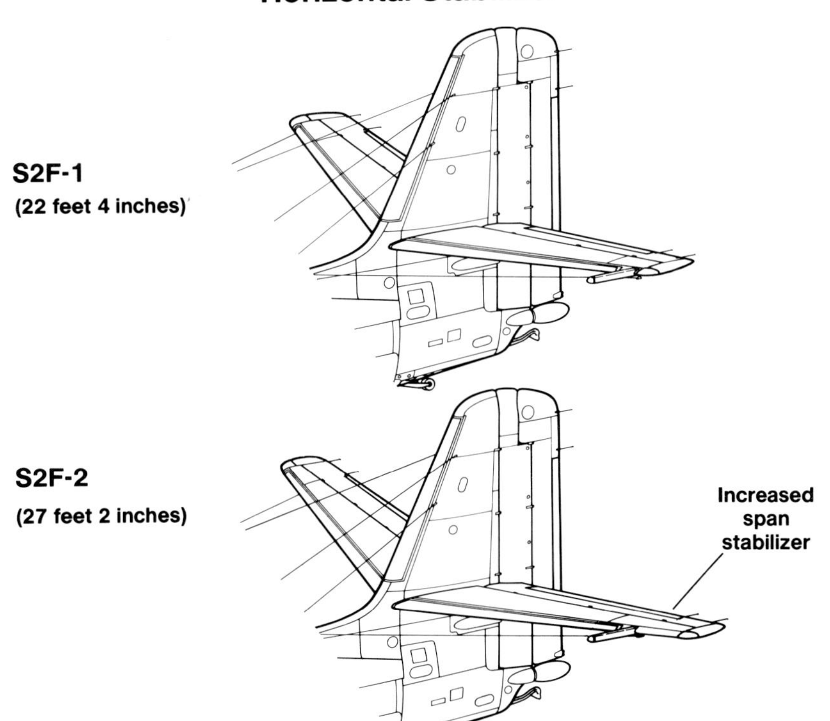

An S2F-2 (BuNo 133349) of VS-38 is launched from the starboard catapult of the escort carrier USS BADOENG STRAIT (CVE-116) on 23 September 1954. (U.S. Navy via Hal Andrews)

This S2F-2 (BuNo 133385) of VS-21 is parked on the Marston matting apron of NAS Oakland on 14 January 1959. The squadron marking on the engine nacelle is a Red lightning bolt on a White field. The underwing pylons are White as are all codes and service markings. (Doug Olson via Pete Bowers)

An S2F-2 (BuNo 133342) of VS-39 launched from the flight deck of USS LEYTE while the ship was operating in the choppy North Atlantic for a series of ASW exercises held in September of 1957. (U.S. Navy via Hal Andrews)

This S2F-2 (BuNo 133370) of VS-21 is sitting on all five wheels, with the tail bumper resting on the ramp. The standard Glossy Sea Blue paint scheme was carried on U.S. Naval aircraft from late 1944 until 1957. (Pete Bowers Collection)

An S2F-2 of VS-22 gets a thorough checkout by plane captains C.W. Mayes, J.R. Waken and L.B. MacDonald at NAS Key West, Florida, on 27 March 1956. The crew entry hatch is open and the boarding ladder is in position below the open door. (U.S. Navy via Hal Andrews)

US-2C

Of the sixty S-2C Trackers produced by Grumman, forty-eight were eventually modified to the US-2C target-towing configuration. The US-2C had all ASW gear including the upper and lower radomes, MAD boom, and wing-mounted searchlight deleted and had a target-tow kit installed in the space formerly taken up by the belly radome. Unlike the earlier US-2A and US-2B, the US-2C engine nacelles were not faired over.

During 1964, the US-2C Tracker replaced the UB-26 (JD-1) Invader as the primary surface-to-air gunnery target tow aircraft in the Pacific Fleet. Target towing is a somewhat dangerous operation and US-2C Tracker crews sometimes thought of themselves as a flying shooting gallery. The tow target was some twenty-three feet long and was towed well behind the Tracker on a long cable. The target sleeve offered the ships and aircraft of the fleet practice in the task of destroying aerial targets.

In addition to the target-towing duties, the US-2C was utilized as an airborne radar target and carried out simulated intercept and attack mission profiles to train ground radar and shipboard Combat Information Center (CIC) personnel.

By October of 1981, all US-2C aircraft had been phased out and retired from the U.S. Navy. The US-2Cs were the most colorfully-marked Trackers in the Navy, normally carrying bright markings consisting of an Engine Gray fuselage, Yellow wings/horizontal stabilizers, a Red vertical stabilizer and Red wing bands.

This US-2C (BuNo 133347) of VC-5, landing at NAS Atsugi, Japan, during 1973, carried colorful tail markings that consisted of a Yellow and Red/Orange checkerboard design that extended past the rudder hinge line. (Hideki Nagakubo)

This US-2C (BuNo 133363) of VU-2 was painted in target towing markings that consisted of an Engine Gray fuselage with Yellow wings and horizontal stabilizers, a Red vertical fin and Red wing stripes. The lettering was Black on the lighter colors and White on the fuselage. The Tracker was based at NAS Quonset Point during June of 1964. (U.S. Navy via Bill Curry)

This US-2C (BuNo 133359) of VC-4 served with a squadron detachment assigned to NAS Cecil Field, Florida, on 25 May 1967. All ASW equipment was removed from the US-2C to provide space for the target towing equipment. (Clay Jansson)

This US-2C (BuNo 133386) of VC-10 was used as a target-tow plane by NAS Guantanamo (GITMO), Cuba to provide aerial and fleet gunnery practice during 1972. The Tracker towed a twenty-three foot target sleeve on a long cable. (U.S. Navy via Peter Mersky Collection)

A US-2C (BuNo 133348) of VU-10 parked on the transient ramp at NAF Washington, DC, during 1972. The US-2C was a modification of the S-2C (S2F-2) with the searchlight, belly-radome and internal ASW equipment removed. (Bob Esposito via Clay Jansson)

Parked on the flight line of NAS North Island, California, on 21 September 1975, a US-2C (BuNo 133358) of VC-1 displays the Black Hawaiian Warrior squadron marking on the outboard sides of both engine nacelles. (Bob Lawson/The Hook)

S2F-2P (RS-2C)

The U.S. Navy modified the 13th production S-2C Tracker (BuNo 133341) to the photo reconnaissance role under the designation S2F-2P (RS-2C). This aircraft was a one-of-a-kind modification which was carried out at NAS Pensacola, Florida, during 1964. Essentially, the Tracker had a bulged camera compartment installation in the rear fuselage to house two camera stations. A total of six aerial cameras were mounted in the fuselage section, two in the forward section just under the cockpit and four in the rear section, two on either side of the fuselage. The two rear most cameras were mounted behind sliding camera port doors in the fuselage sides.

Although the RS-2C proved to be a serviceable camera platform, the Navy had successfully developed a standard underwing pylon mounted camera pod for the S-2. It was felt that further conversions of the Tracker to the photo reconnaissance role were unnecessary, since any S2F could be configured as a photographic aircraft with the simple installation of a camera pod on one or more of the underwing pylons.

This RS-2C (S2F-2P/BuNo 133341) of VU-3 on the ramp at NAS North Island California, on 14 February 1970, was a one-of-a-kind modification that consisted of six aerial cameras installed in an S2F-2 (S-2C) airframe. This aircraft was modified by the Navy, not Grumman, as a test platform. (Clay Jansson)

The RS-2C was also flown by VX-1 before it was retired to the storage facility at Davis Monthan AFB, near Phoenix, AZ. VX-1 was part of the Navy's Operational Test and Evaluation Force. (Clay Jansson)

Camera Installation

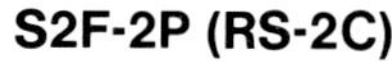

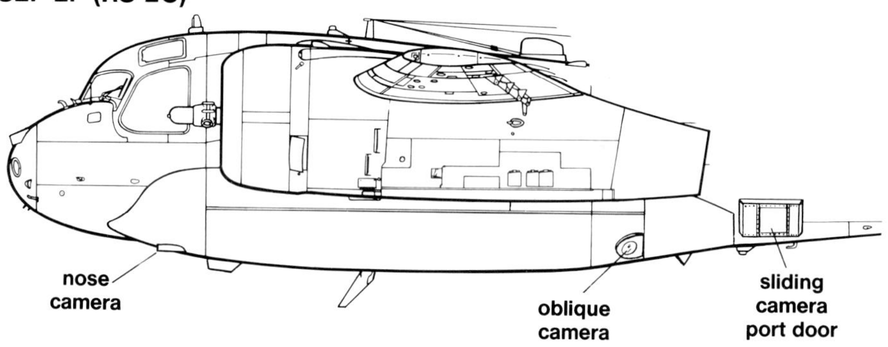

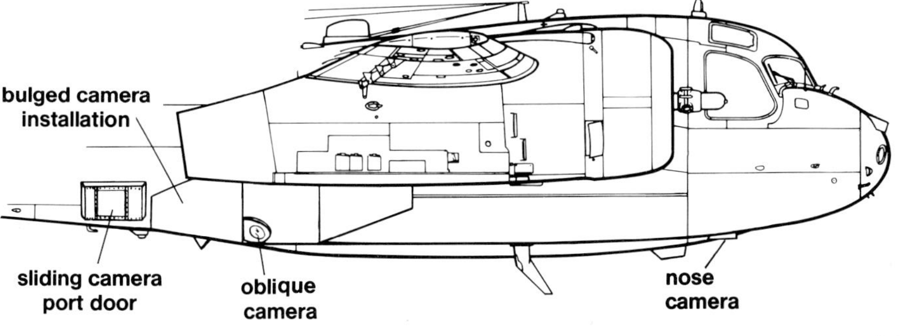

S2F-3 (S-2D)

The S2F-3 (S-2D) was the third and final airframe design change in the S-2 Tracker line. Grumman manufactured 100 aircraft and this variant incorporated some major structural changes. When the S2F-3 (S-2D) entered service with the U.S. Navy during October of 1960, it allowed the Navy to retire the majority of the remaining S2F-1s, with most leaving service by the end of 1961.

The S2F-3 (S-2D) incorporated the most modern developments in airborne ASW electronics available, including updated JULIE and JEZEBEL equipment, along with increased armament capability. It looked and listened for enemy submarines with powerful radar and sonobuoys, echo ranging explosive charges and MAD gear.

The S2F-3 differed from the earlier S2F-1 and S2F-2 in a number of ways. The APA-69 ECM direction finder radome over the cockpit was deleted. With the reduction in the size of ASW weapons, the enlarged weapons bay of the S2F-2 was no longer necessary and the fuselage was returned to the shape of the earlier S2F-1. The rear of each engine nacelle was changed. The "hawkbill" fairing was deleted and the nacelles were enlarged to increase the sonobuoy capacity from eight on the S2F-1 to sixteen on the S2F-3 (S-2D), for a total capacity of thirty-two sonobuoys. The S2F-3 featured uprated R1820-82A engines which required the engine air intake on the upper engine nacelle to be enlarged.

By a rearrangement of internal equipment, the fuselage crew compartment section was increased eighteen inches in length and 3.35 inches in width. This gave the crew additional room and allowed for an increase in internal fuel capacity. With the additional fuel, the S2F-3/S-2D could remain on station for seven and one half hours, over an hour longer than earlier versions.

To give the Tracker increased lift to compensate for its higher gross weight, the wingspan was increased by three feet. The wingtips were also changed from the squared off tips of the earlier S2F variants to a rounded wingtip which featured built-in ECM antennas. The underwing pylons were strengthened to allow for the carriage of heavier ordnance loads including ASW torpedos. For quieter ASW equipment operation, the S-2D electrical system was changed from DC to AC power. The larger horizontal tail, first installed on the S2F-2 (S-2C), was retained on the S2F-3.

The first pre-production S2F-3 (BuNo 147531) made its first flight on 20 May 1959. Carrier trials were held aboard the USS INTREPID and USS KEARSARGE during the late Spring/early Summer of 1960. The first delivery of a production S2F-3 to a fleet squadron was made to VS-36 at NAS Norfolk, Virginia, on 26 October 1960.

The S2F-3/S-2D has the distinction of being the only reported combat loss of a Tracker. During the early morning of 21 January 1968, an S-2D (BuNo 149252) of VS-35, operating from the USS HORNET, was lost off the coast of Vietnam. The Tracker was returning to the carrier after a night surveillance mission when it disappeared off the HORNET's radar screen approximately 100 miles from the ship. Although an extensive Search and Rescue effort was mounted, no trace of the S-2D or its crew was ever found.

This S2F-3 (S-2D/BuNo 147531) is carrying two ASW homing torpedos on the underwing pylons. The S2F-3 had strengthened pylons which could handle heavier loads than the earlier S2Fs. The S2F-3 also featured rounded wingtips with built in ECM antennas and larger airscoops on the engine nacelles. (Grumman via Terry Panopalis)

Fuselage/Nacelle Development

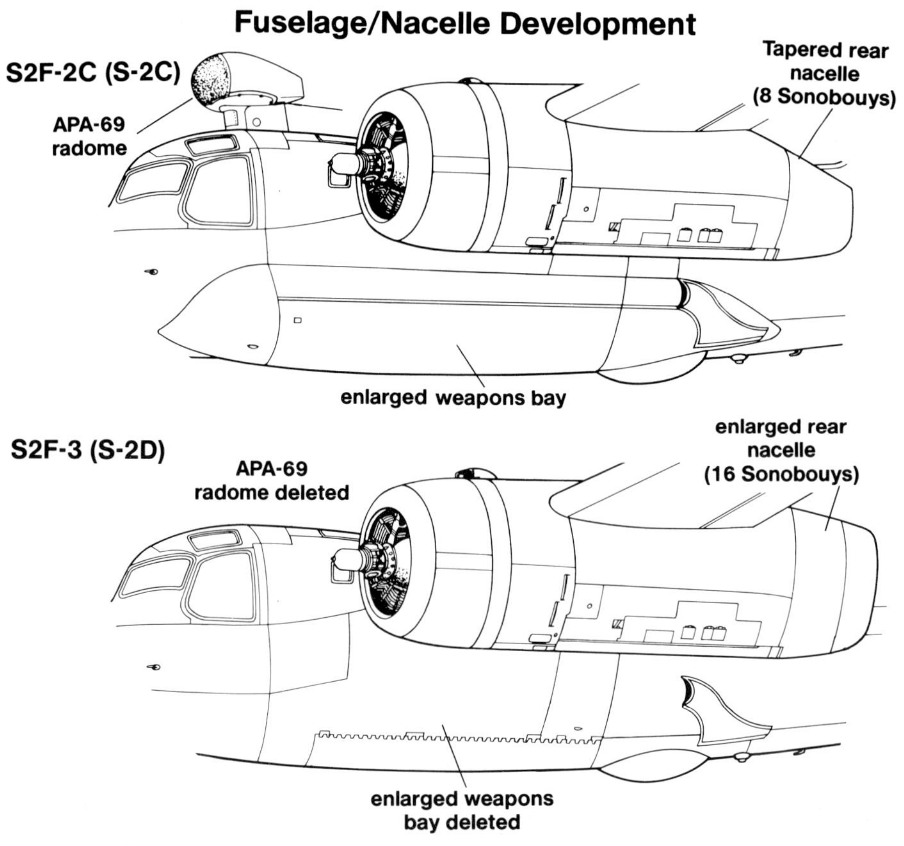

This S-2D (BuNo 147868) was assigned to the U.S. Navy Test Pilot School at the Naval Air Test Center, NAS Patuxent River, Maryland, on 15 July 1968. The Tracker possessed flying characteristics that qualified it to be in the group of different aircraft types routinely flown by TPS pilots. (Bob Esposito)

An S-2D (BuNo 148717), attached to the Reserve Unit at NAS Alameda, California, sits on the deserted ramp at Greenville-Spartanburg Jetport in South Carolina on 28 January 1968. The crew entry door is open and the boarding ladder is in place. (Jim Sullivan)

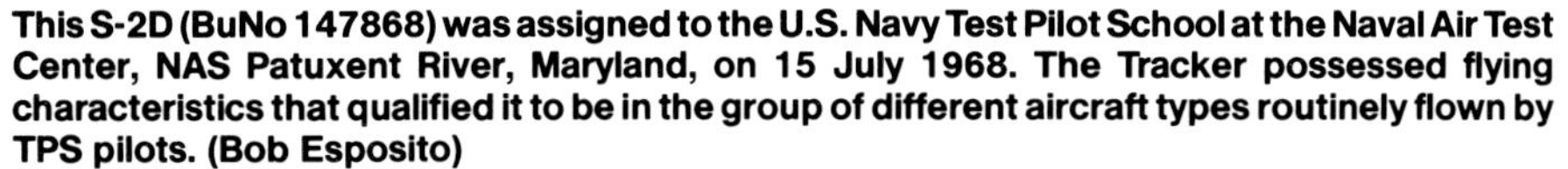
An S-2D (S3F-3/BuNo 147882) of VS-36 takes a waveoff from the LSO aboard USS RANDOLPH during 1965. VS-36 was attached to Carrier Anti-Submarine Warfare Group (CVSG) 58. The squadron marking on the rudder was a Yellow lightning bolt outlined in Black. (Grumman)

Engine Cowling

S2F-2
(S-2C)

S2F-3
(S-2D)

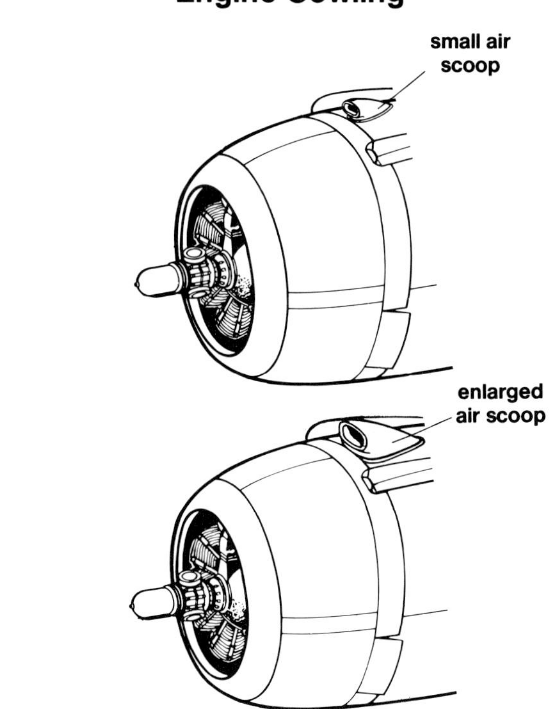

The large White object in the center of the main instrument panel is a plotting board, which is covering the radar repeater scope.

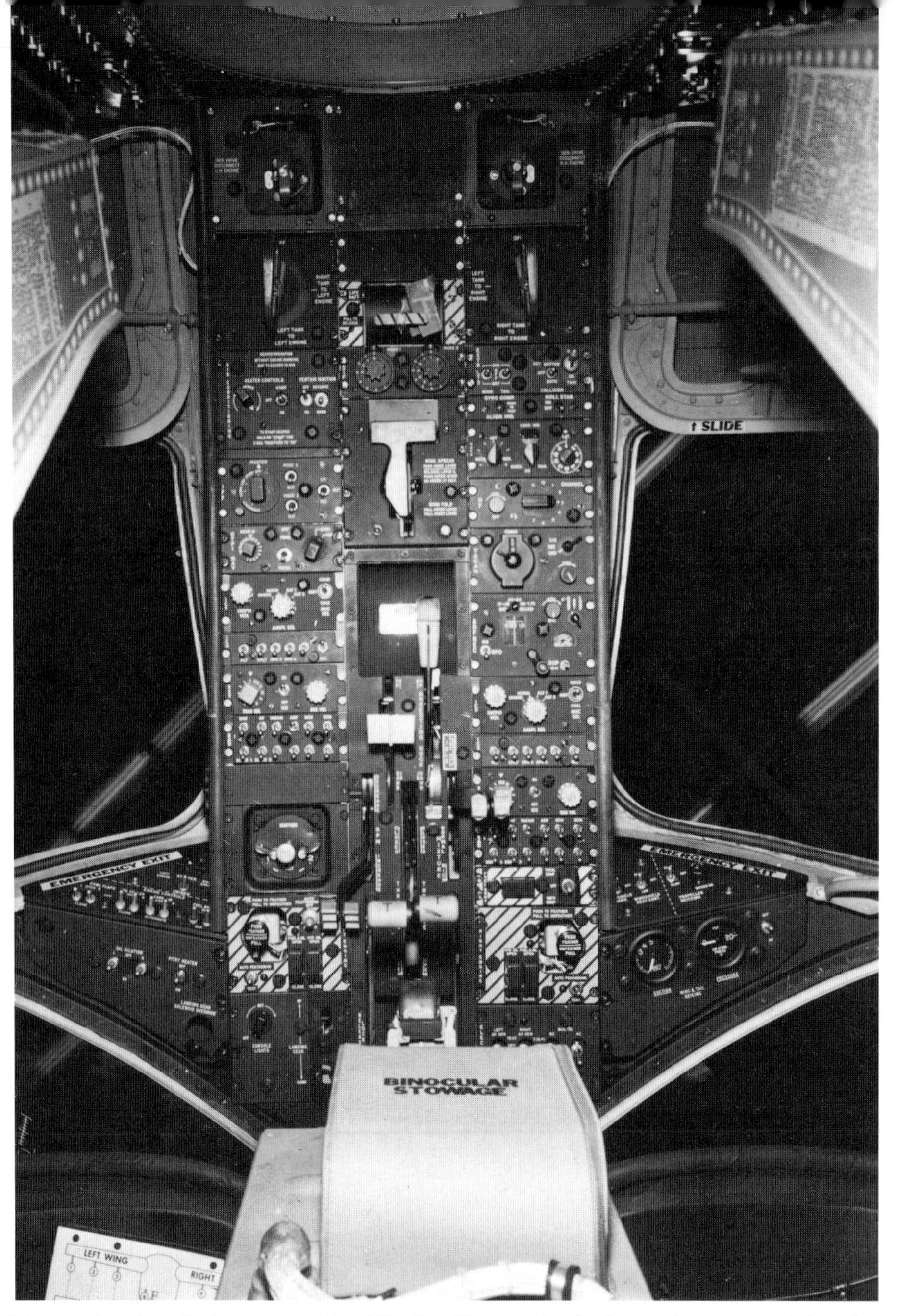

The overhead control panel contained the throttles, engine instruments and a container for holding binoculars.

The port ASW Operator's Station contained the main search radar screen and other sensor equipment.

The starboard ASW Operator's Station had the plotting tape printer for the MAD system and the sonobuoy release control panel (far right).

S-2D (148728) of VS-934, a Reserve unit at NAS Willow Grove, PA, parked on the air station's concrete ramp on 8 April 1970. The longer, rounded wingtips on the S-2D housed ECM antennas. (Roger F. Besecker)

Tied down to the deck of USS RANDOLPH, while visiting Portsmouth, England, during July of 1966, this S-2D (BuNo 148744) of VS-34 carries a Yellow fin tip as a squadron marking. The wing fold is covered with a waterproof protective cover to protect it from the weather. (Peter Russell-Smith)

Wing Tip

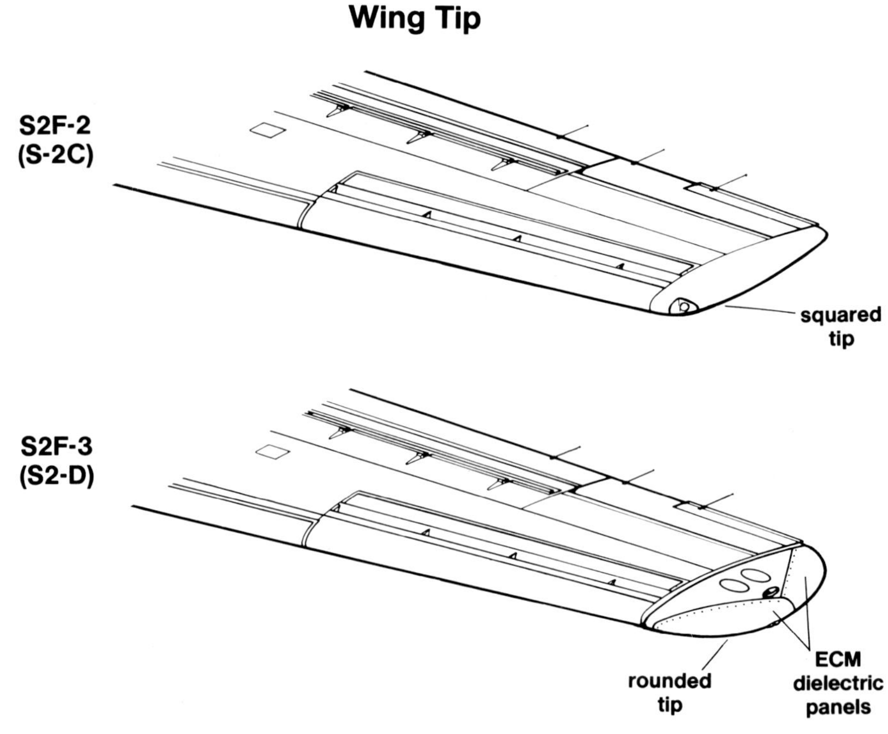

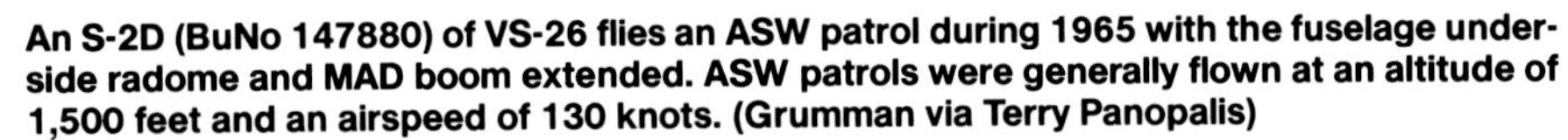
An S-2D (BuNo 147880) of VS-26 flies an ASW patrol during 1965 with the fuselage underside radome and MAD boom extended. ASW patrols were generally flown at an altitude of 1,500 feet and an airspeed of 130 knots. (Grumman via Terry Panopalis)

US-2D

A total of fifty-four S2F-3 (S-2D) airframes were modified as utility/training aircraft under the designation US-2D. This version was a utility and training aircraft and flew exclusively with the U.S. Navy. Unlike the three earlier utility variants (US-2A, -2B, -2C), the US-2D retained the belly-mounted radome; however, all internal ASW equipment was removed. Although the searchlight assembly was retained on the wing, its internal parts were deleted. Neither the belly radome or searchlight nacelle was faired over.

ES-2D

Seven S-2D airframes were converted to the electronics role under the designation ES-2D. These aircraft carried additional electronics equipment and most served as range-clearing aircraft for Navy missile test ranges such as Point Mugu, California. A number of ES-2Ds had an additional search radar radome installed on the forward underside of the fuselage. In addition to its mission of range-clearing, ES-2Ds also functioned in an Airborne Early Warning (AEW) training role.

The last ES-2D flight occurred in March of 1986, as the last STOOF left the Pacific Missile Range Facility and was retired from the U.S. Navy. The aircraft's last flight was to the Davis-Monthan storage facility in Arizona.

This US-2D (BuNo 147880) was assigned to NAS North Island, California, during October of 1970. The Black lines painted on the rear of the engine nacelle are flap-deflection marks. A fuel dump pipe extends from the rear starboard side of the nacelle and although the searchlight pod is in place, the internal parts have been removed. (Clay Jansson)

A US-2D (BuNo 149229), with its wings folded to conserve space, is parked on the ramp at NAS Quonset Point, RI, during August of 1971. The MAD boom, searchlight assembly and ASW gear have been removed. The empty belly radome has been left in place rather than fairing it over. (Lionel Paul)

An ES-2D (BuNo 147872) assigned to the Pacific Missile Range at Point Mugu, California, during October of 1975. The aircraft carried powerful speakers mounted on the outboard wing pylon to warn boaters of an impending missile launch. (Peter Mancus)

S2F-3S (S-2E)

The S2F-3S (S-2E) was an improved version of the S2F-3 (S-2D) and the last production variant of the S2F to be built by Grumman. A total of 252 were manufactured, with 238 seeing service with the U.S. Navy and fourteen being exported to Australia.

The S2F-3S (S-2E) differed externally from the S2F-3 by the addition of an antenna bulge under the rear fuselage just behind the retractable belly radome and the addition of a long, retractable blade antenna on the underside of the fuselage which ran parallel to the weapons bay hinge line.

The major internal change between the S-2D and S-2E was the installation of the ASN-30 Automated Tactical Navigation Equipment system. This system replaced the ASA-13 plotter, the navigational computer and the ASA-31 Julie computer. This equipment change brought the gross weight of the S-2E to 29,150 pounds, some 3,150 pounds heavier than the S2F-1. The F-1 autopilot of earlier S-2 variants was replaced by the MA-67 autopilot, which maintained both altitude and heading. Improvements in the MAD gear more than doubled the detection range over that of the S2F-1 (S-2A). The larger, 728 gallon, fuel capacity of the S-2E increased the aircraft's endurance to eight hours. As a safety feature, the aircraft was equipped with an improved fuel dump system which allowed the internal fuel load to be jettisoned more quickly.

The S2F-3S (S-2E) was capable of speeds in excess of 200 knots (230 mph) and could reach an altitude of 20,000 feet. The 85 million candlepower searchlight (carbon arc) would effectively illuminate a submarine snorkle one mile away from an altitude of 300 feet. On patrol missions, the S-2E normally cruised at 130 knots at an altitude of 1,500 feet.

The S-2E first entered fleet service with VS-41 during 1962 and the type remained in service until the early 1970s when they were replaced by the last of the S-2 series, the S-2G.

An S-2E (BuNo 152839) of VS-38 has its MAD gear, retractable blade antenna and retractable radome extended for a search mission on 8 March 1972. NT-301 was operating from NAS North Island, San Diego, California. (Bob Lawson/The Hook)

S-2Es of VS-27 on the flight line of NAS Rota, Spain, during April of 1972. VS-27 was attached to CVSG-56 aboard the USS INTREPID. One of the identification features of the S-2E was the second smaller belly mounted radome just behind the retractable radome. (U.S. Navy via Peter Mersky Collection)

A rarely seen marking on S-2s was this sharkmouth design carried on an S-2E (BuNo 153572) of VS-24. The mismatched mouth indicates that the nose cap was a replacement from another sharkmouthed Tracker. VS-24 was part of CVSG-56 aboard the USS INTREPID during the ship's visit to Portsmouth, England, in September of 1971. (Peter Russell-Smith)

This S-2E (BuNo 149892) of VS-23 on the ramp at NAS North Island on 2 May 1964, carries the special markings used during UNITAS-23, a large-scale military exercise held with South American countries. The nose stripes, XXIII on the nacelle and the outline above and below the Black Panther on the fin tip are RED. (Clay Jansson)

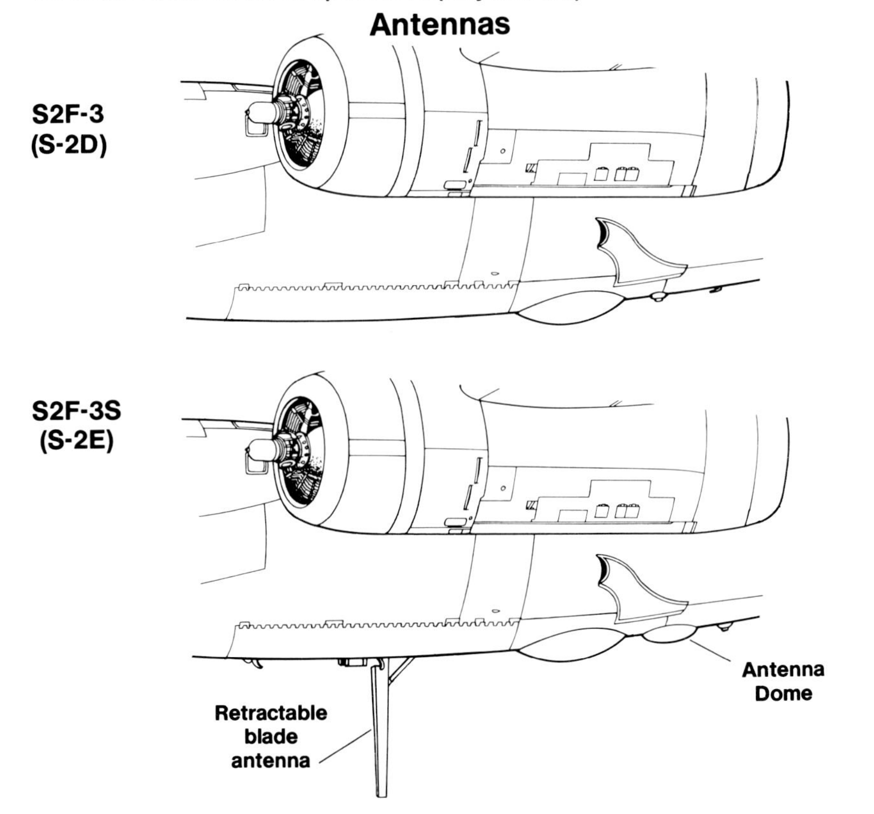

This S-2E (BuNo 151640) of VS-25 is armed with six 5 inch HVAR rockets on the underwing pylons. The small second radome on the fuselage underside behind the belly radome identifies this STOOF as an S-2E. (U.S. Navy via Peter Mersky Collection)

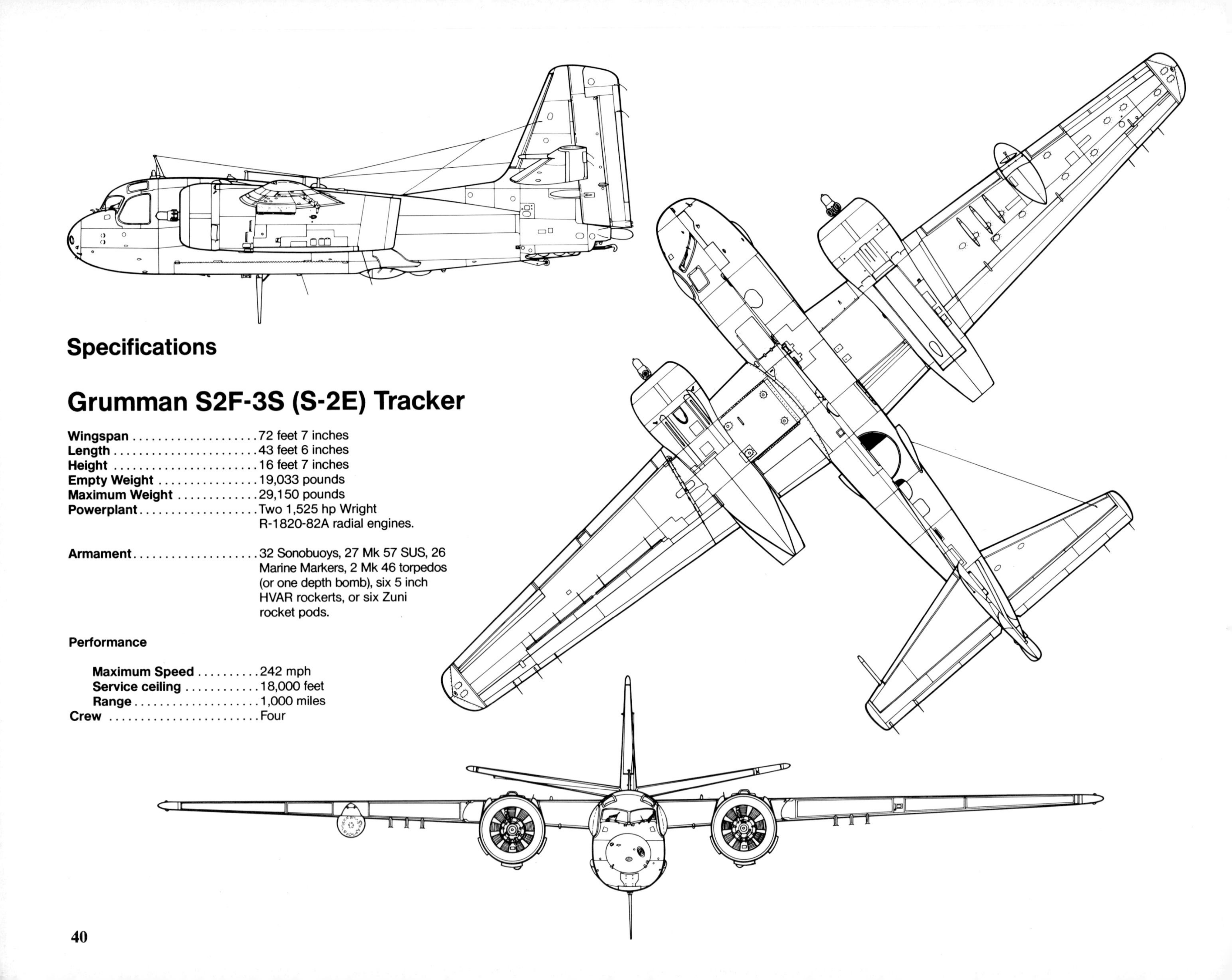

Specifications

Grumman S2F-3S (S-2E) Tracker

Wingspan .... 72 feet 7 inches
Length .... 43 feet 6 inches
Height .... 16 feet 7 inches
Empty Weight .... 19,033 pounds
Maximum Weight .... 29,150 pounds
Powerplant .... Two 1,525 hp Wright R-1820-82A radial engines.

Armament .... 32 Sonobuoys, 27 Mk 57 SUS, 26 Marine Markers, 2 Mk 46 torpedos (or one depth bomb), six 5 inch HVAR rockerts, or six Zuni rocket pods.

Performance

Maximum Speed .... 242 mph
Service ceiling .... 18,000 feet
Range .... 1,000 miles
Crew .... Four

This S-2E (BuNo 149263) of VS-41 on the ramp at NAS North Island during May of 1967, had a combination camera pod/flare launcher on the outboard pylon and a Mk 46 practice torpedo on the inboard pylon. The squadron markings are Green shamrocks on a White rudder. (Author's Collection)

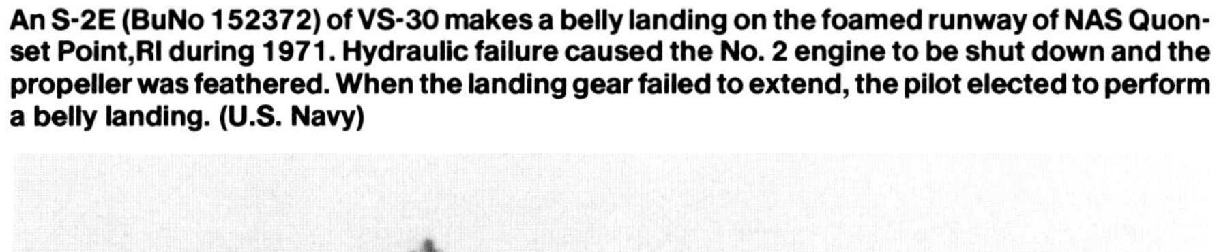

An S-2E (BuNo 152372) of VS-30 makes a belly landing on the foamed runway of NAS Quonset Point, RI during 1971. Hydraulic failure caused the No. 2 engine to be shut down and the propeller was feathered. When the landing gear failed to extend, the pilot elected to perform a belly landing. (U.S. Navy)

An S-2E (BuNo 152339) of VS-37 unleashes Zuni rockets over the Chocolate Mountain Aerial Weapons Testing Range located near Yuma, AZ, on 24 June 1978. The rockets were carried in four shot LAU-10A launcher pods and the S-2E could carry six such pods. (U.S. Navy via Peter Mersky Collection)

An S-2E of VS-33 is given the signal to spread wings by plane captain Edwin L. Larkin on the ramp at NAS North Island, during February 1970. The squadron insignia is carried beneath the cockpit on both sides of the aircraft and the squadron code/aircraft number are carried on the upper wing in Black. (U.S. Navy via Robert Dorr)

S-2G

The S-2G was the final variant of the S-2 series to see service with the U.S. Navy. The S-2G was not a production aircraft but rather a rebuild program involving sixty S-2E airframes, modified with new electronics. The first S-2G was delivered in December of 1972 and went to VS-37 based at NAS North Island, California. VS-37 used the S-2G during its WESTPAC deployments onboard the USS KITTY HAWK during 1973 and 1975.

The S-2G featured updated ASW equipment, in the form of the AN/AQA-7 DIFAR processing equipment which more efficiently handled sonobuoy transmitted information. This equipment was the same installation which had been installed on the P-3 Orion. Externally, the S-2G differed from the earlier S-2E in the installation of a three-tube smoke marker retro-ejector mounted on the starboard side of the starboard engine nacelle.

The S-2G modification program was carried out by Navy personnel using kits provided by the Baltimore division of the Martin-Marietta Corp. The actual modification work was handled by the Naval Air Rework Facility (NARF) at NAS Quonset Point, Rhode Island. The S-2G was destined to serve longer than originally intended, while fleet squadrons transitioned to the Lockheed S-3 Viking. The Navy wanted to have a proven aircraft, the S-2G Tracker, flying with operational fleet units as the S-3 Vikings were being phased into the ASW role. As the number of operational S-3 squadrons increased, the S-2Gs were withdrawn from service and retired. In August of 1977, the last S-2G (BuNo 152374) of VS-37, was officially retired and made its final flight to the Davis-Monthan AFB storage facility.

This S-2G (BuNo 152816) of VS-37 on the ramp at NAS North Island on 27 March 1976, has a smoke marker retro-ejector pod installed on the starboard side of the engine nacelle. The pod carried three marine smoke markers. The S-2G was the last S-2 variant to serve with the U.S. Navy. (Clay Jansson)

This Atlantic Fleet S-2G (BuNo 152378) of VS-28 stationed at NAS Quonset Point, RI, during 1971. The 'AT' on the rudder was Black outlined with Red and the squadron chevron marking on the tail was Yellow, White and Black. (Lionel Paul)

Smoke Marker Retro-Ejector

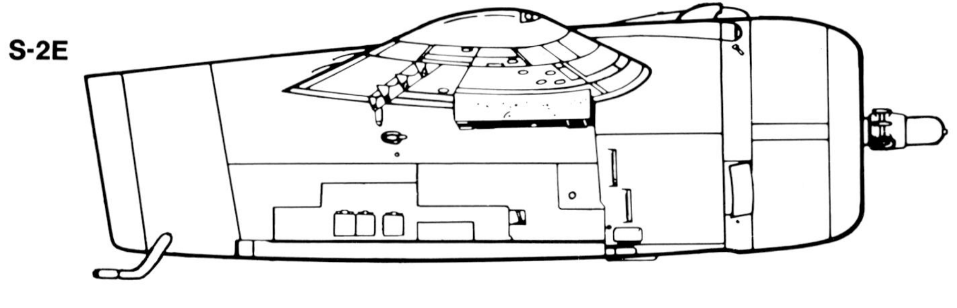

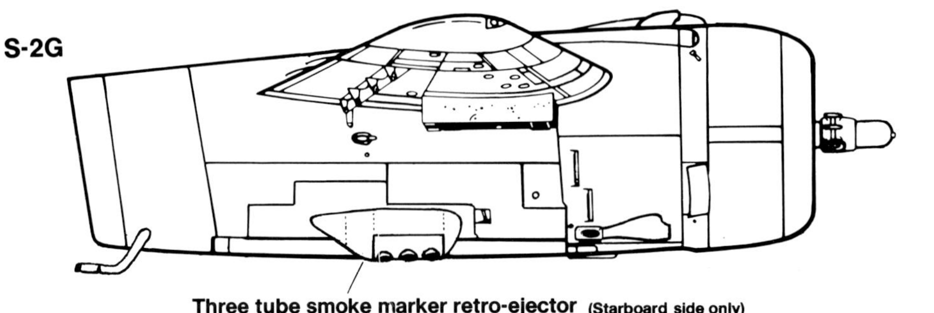

An S-2G (BuNo 152345) of VS-33 on the ramp at NAS North Island on 22 September 1973. VS-33 was assigned to Carrier Air Wing 11 (CVW-11) on board USS KITTY HAWK (CV-63). NH-017 has not yet been fitted with the smoke marker retro-ejector installation on the engine nacelle. (Peter Mancus)

This S-2G (BuNo 152374) of VS-37 belonged to CVSG-59 and flew from the USS TICONDEROGA during March of 1973. When shore based between deployments, the squadron flew from NAS North Island, California. The fin cap was Yellow and the rudder had Black sunrays outlined in Yellow. (Peter Mancus)

This YS-2G (BuNo 152333) was assigned to the Naval Research Laboratory during February of 1977. The lettering within the Kangaroo on the rear fuselage reads: "1977 SST Approved." The series of letters and numbers on the nose under the aircraft number refers to the code for storage at Davis-Monthan AFB, AZ. (Clay Jansson)

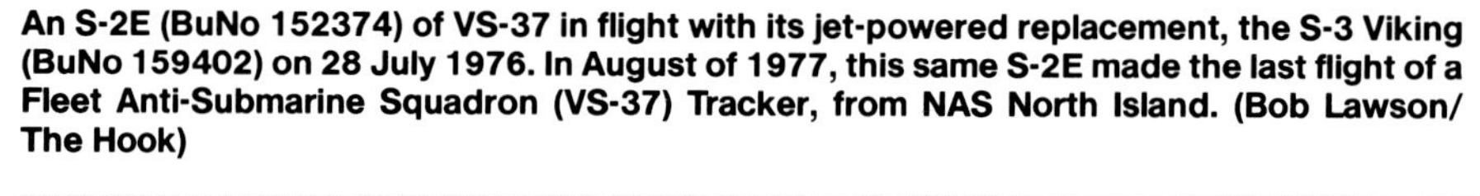
An S-2E (BuNo 152374) of VS-37 in flight with its jet-powered replacement, the S-3 Viking (BuNo 159402) on 28 July 1976. In August of 1977, this same S-2E made the last flight of a Fleet Anti-Submarine Squadron (VS-37) Tracker, from NAS North Island. (Bob Lawson/ The Hook)

Foreign Trackers

The S-2 series was widely exported under the Mutual Defense Assistance Program. Australia received eighteen Trackers direct from Grumman, while Argentina, Brazil, Italy, Japan, the Netherlands, Peru, South Korea, Taiwan, Thailand, Turkey, Uruguay, and Venezuela all received Trackers from U.S. Navy stocks. Additionally a number of Canadian-built Trackers were also exported.

Overseas, the Tracker served in both the ASW and maritime surveillance role. Some nations, such as Argentina, the Netherlands, Brazil and Australia operated the Trackers from aircraft carriers, while others used the S-2 as a land based ASW/patrol aircraft. South Korean Trackers were used primarily as patrol aircraft in the anti-infiltration boat role.

The Tracker continues to be operated by a number of these countries and at least three are considering service life extension programs aimed at extending the life of the Tracker well into the 1990s and beyond. Taiwan and Brazil are in the process of rendering contracts to re-engine their Trackers with turboprop engines as well as upgrading the electronics on their S-2s.

Dutch Navy S-2Ns (modified S-2As) carried a two tone Gray camouflage scheme. The S-2N was a version of the S2F-1 (S-2A) modified for use by the Netherlands Navy by Fairey of Canada. This Tracker was landing at Ypenberg, Holland during 1970. (M. Herben)

This S-2E (BuNo 153595) was one of fourteen built by Grumman for direct export to Australia. The Trackers eventually equipped four squadrons of the Australian Navy and deployed aboard the Australian aircraft carrier HMAS MELBOURNE. (Grumman)

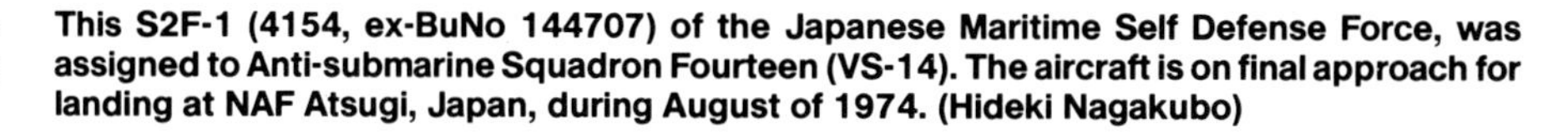

This S2F-1 (4154, ex-BuNo 144707) of the Japanese Maritime Self Defense Force, was assigned to Anti-submarine Squadron Fourteen (VS-14). The aircraft is on final approach for landing at NAF Atsugi, Japan, during August of 1974. (Hideki Nagakubo)

An S2F-1 (BuNo 136659) of the Republic of Korea Air Force is parked on the ramp at Pittsburg, PA, during December of 1971. The color scheme is Gloss Gull Gray uppersurfaces over Gloss Black undersurfaces. (D. Barnes via JEM Aviation Slides)

This S-2E (BuNo 149878) was one of eight aircraft acquired by Venezuela from the U.S. Navy. The aircraft were operated by Esuadron Aeronaval Anti-submarine No. 1 at Puerto Cabello, Venezuela, during 1974. These aircraft reportedly still remain in service. (Bill Sides)

This S-2A (A-851, ex-BuNo 133215) was one of three S-2As delivered to the Uruguayan Navy and based at Punta Del Este during February of 1965. During its delivery flight to Uruguay, the Tracker carried both American and Uruguayan markings. (via Bob Lawson/The Hook)

The S-2 was used by both the Korean Air Force and Navy. This S-2E (BuNo 149264), at NAS Dallas, Tx, during July of 1976, belonged to the Korean Navy and was one of twenty-three aircraft provided for ASW and coastal patrol work. The Tracker carried the standard Gull Gray over White paint scheme. (D. Barnes via JEM Aviation Slides)

Turbo-Tracker

Marsh Aviation of Mesa, Arizona, developed the first turboprop conversion of the S-2 airframe during 1986. These aircraft were intended for the fire fighting role for the California Forestry Department. The Marsh conversion consisted of removal of all ASW related equipment from surplus S-2 airframes, installation of a fire retardant tank in the weapons bay, and re-engining with 1,712 shp Garrett TPE331-14 turboprop engines driving five blade Hartzell propellers.

With the new engines, the S-2 has a 69 mph higher cruising speed with a fifty percent reduction in fuel consumption and a thirty percent reduction in takeoff and landing runs.

With the success of the Marsh conversion, other turboprop conversion programs aimed at the military market are being undertaken. During February of 1989, IPM of Canada received a contract to convert eleven S-2s for the Brazilian Navy with Pratt & Whitney PT6A-67 turboprops. This contract is in addition to the work being done by IMP for the Canadian Armed Forces.

Grumman has received a $260 million contract to modify thirty-two S-3E Trackers to the S-2T Turbo Tracker configuration for supply to Taiwan under a Navy administered FMS contract. The S-2T differs from the Turbo Tracker conversions in that it uses the 1,645 shp Garrett TPE331-1-5AW turboprop engine driving a four blade Rotol propeller.

Several other countries are currently considering converting their Trackers to the Turboprop configuration, with the majority of these projects at present depending on finding the necessary funding.

S2F-1 (S-2A/BuNo 136613/N426DF) has been modified with a turboprop engine by Marsh Aviation of Mesa, AZ. Powered by a Garrett TPE331-14 turboprop driving a five blade Hartzell propeller, this Turbo-Tracker is configured as a firefighter for the California Division of Forestry (CDF) during 1988. (Marsh Aviation Co.)

This S-2T *TurboTracker* is one of thirty-two aircraft being modified by Grumman for Taiwan under a U. S. Navy administered FMS contract. The aircraft are powered by 1,645 shp turboprop engines, have new avionics and updated ASW systems. (Grumman)

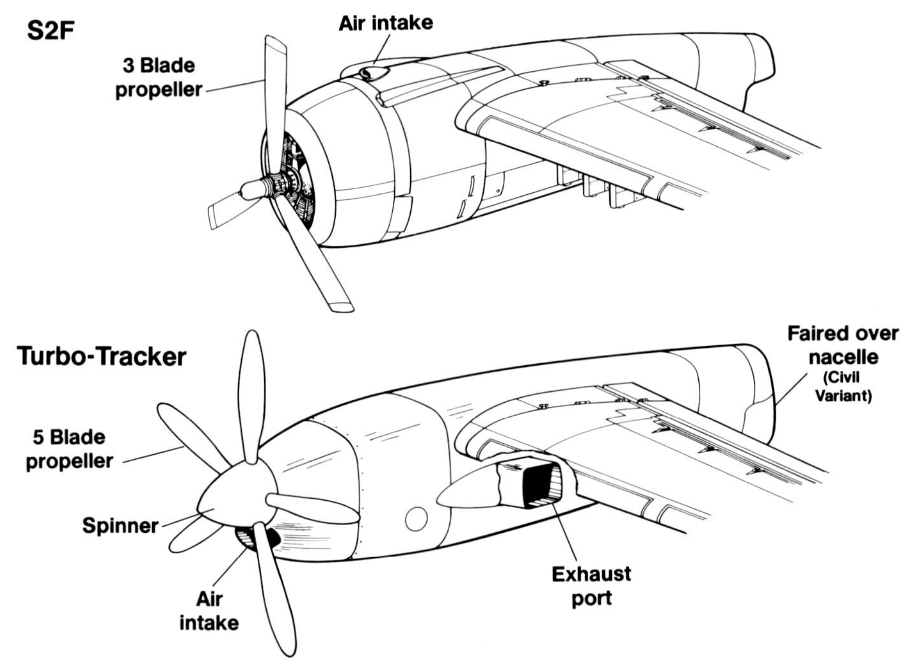

TF-1 (C-1A)

During 1954 Grumman began work on a dedicated cargo/passenger variant of the S2F under the company designation, Model G-96. The aircraft was intended to replace the TBM-3R as the Navy's Carrier Onboard Delivery (COD) aircraft.

The G-96 was given the Navy designation TF-1 Trader and made its first flight on 19 January 1955. It was powered by the 1,525 hp Wright R-1820-82 engines, the same powerplants installed in the standard S2F-1. The TF-1 differed from the S2F-1 in having a deepened fuselage, giving the TF-1 a whale-like belly profile. The rear of the engine nacelles were faired over and windows were installed in the fuselage sides. The passenger compartment had a capacity for nine rearward-facing seats, which could easily be removed to convert the aircraft over for hauling cargo.

The auto-pilot equipped TF-1 (C-1A) was considered an all-weather aircraft and was also used as both a multi-engine trainer and/or instrument trainer. The Trader also performed carrier qualification flights for multi-engine pilots. A total of eighty-seven TF-1 (C-1A) Traders were built by Grumman exclusively for the U.S. Navy.

Four C-1A airframes were modified by Grumman to become TF-1Q (EC-1A) aircraft (BuNos 136783, 785, 787 and 788). This variant functioned as a Electronics Counter Measures (ECM) aircraft and its mission was to disrupt communications and confuse enemy ECM and Radar systems. It was used exclusively to train aircraft, ship and land-based crews in determining the capabilities and/or limitations of their active and passive ECM gear. The modification consisted of removal of the passenger seats and the installation of an ECM suite consisting of jamming transmitters, noise modulators, chaff dispensers, extra antennas and underwing ECM pods. This equipment was used to jam simulated 'enemy' receiving facilities.

The C-1A was known in WESTPAC as the "Mailman of the Fleet" and many Traders saw service during the Vietnam War flying mail, personnel and cargo on and off the carriers. After serving the U.S. Navy for some thirty-five years, the last operational C-1A Trader (BuNo 146048) was retired from service on 30 September 1988.

One of four TF-1Q (EC-1A/BuNo 136787) Traders assigned to VAW-11 rests between missions during 1959. The ECM pods on the underwing pylons and antennas on the fuselage gave the Trader a powerful jamming capability. 'RR-799' was eventually converted back to standard C-1A configuration. (Pete Bowers Collection)

This C-1A (BuNo 136782) of VX-5 carries Bi-Centennial markings consisting of a Red-White-Blue flag painted on the entire length of the engine nacelle. The lettering *VAMPIRE AIRLINES* is in Black and refers to the squadron name, the Vampires. (Clay Jansson)

A C-1A (TF-1/BuNo 136769) assigned to USS KITTY HAWK (CVA-63) as a COD (Carrier Onboard Delivery) aircraft during the ship's Vietnam deployment in October of 1969. The C-1A was used primarily for ferrying passengers and mail to and from the ship. (Bob Lawson/ The Hook)

This C-1A (BuNo 136780) was named *BLUE GHOST* and assigned to USS LEXINGTON during July of 1976. The aircraft carries colorful Bi-Centennial markings including a flag on the forward part of the engine nacelles, a Royal Blue "Casper" and USS LEXINGTON in Yellow on the Insignia Blue rudder. (Carlton Eddy)

WF-2 (E-1B)

To provide the fleet with an Airborne Early Warning (AEW) aircraft designed to detect enemy aircraft and direct fighters to intercept them, Grumman developed the model G-117. The G-117 was basically a TF-1 airframe modified to accept an airborne radar system. The aerodynamic prototype (C-1A BuNo 136792), carrying the large dish shaped antenna above the fuselage, first flew on 17 Decembeı 1956. Tests with this aircraft and three pre-production trials aircraft (BuNos 145957, 958 and 146303) proved successful and the Navy ordered the aircraft into production under the designation WF-2 (E-1B) Tracer. The first production Tracer made its initial flight on 28 February 1958.

The WF-2 (E-1B) Tracer featured a lengthened fuselage some eighteen inches longer than the TF-1 and a modified tail section to support the large radome. The tail section consisted of twin outer fins with a short middle fin. The middle fin served as the rear support for the massive APS-82 radome, mounted on the top of the fuselage by a series of three struts. The WF-2 had many nicknames inspired by its appearance and its designation, such as the "STOOF WITH A ROOF" and the "WILLIE FUDD."

The overhead wing-folding arrangement of the S2F and C-1A, was replaced on the Tracer with a rearward-folding wing similar to those used on the Grumman F4F and F6F of WW II fame. A steerable tailwheel was installed to help maneuver the Tracer on the deck, since the aircraft was somewhat tail-heavy with the wings in the folded position. As with the earlier S2F and C-1A, the WF-2 was powered by 1,525 hp Wright R-1820-82A engines.

When the WF-2 (E-1B) joined the fleet during early 1961, the Tracer soon replaced the remaining Douglas AD-5W (A-1G) Skyraiders as the standard shipboard AEW aircraft. Besides its primary AEW mission, the WF-2 was also used in the sea-search crew training role. When assigned to fleet carriers, WF-2 (E-1B) squadrons usually deployed a four aircraft detachment.

Grumman produced a total of eighty-eight Tracers for the U.S. Navy. These aircraft saw extensive service during the early Vietnam War, providing combat air patrol (CAP) fighters with target vectors, and controlling Alpha Strikes over North Vietnam. With a search radius of some 250-300 miles, the E-1B served as an early warning to strike aircraft of enemy MiG activity. During 1964, the Tracer was joined in fleet service by the Grumman E-2A Hawkeye and by May of 1973, only four Tracers of RVAW-110 at NAS North Island, California remained in service. These were soon retired during mid-Summer of 1973, and were ferried to the Davis-Monthan storage facility.

This E-1B (BuNo 148907) of RVAW-10 had just recovered aboard USS TICONDEROGA, operating off the coast of Boston, Mass., during January of 1972 for day carrier qualification training. (Lionel Paul)

This WF-2 (E-1B/BuNo 147224) of VAW-11 reveals the partially open crew entrance hatch on the port side of the fuselage. The steerable tail wheel locked in forward position when wings were folded and the wing fold on the E-1 differed from the wing fold of the S-2/C-1 series. (Clay Jansson)

An E-1B (BuNo 147229) Tracer of VAW-111 makes touch and go landings at its home station, NAS North Island, California, during August of 1968. This 'Stoof with a roof' operated with CVSG-55 aboard USS YORKTOWN. The squadron markings were White stars on Dark Blue bands on both the tip and bottom of the fin. (Warren M. Bodie)

This E-1B (BuNo 148908) of VAW-121 was assigned to USS INTREPID during her visit to Portsmouth, England, on 11 September 1971. E-1Bs served as AEW (Airborne Early Warning) aircraft providing the fleet with information on incoming enemy aircraft. (Peter Russell-Smith)

An E-1B (BuNo 148914) of VAW-111 over the sea near NAS North Island during 1972. The large dish mounted on top of the Tracer housed the APS-82 search radar antenna and actually contributed to the aircraft's lift. (U.S. Navy via Bill Curry)

This E-1B (BuNo 147219) of VAW-207 was assigned to the reserves as a part of CVWR-20 during November of 1973. The Tracer's home station was NAS Jacksonville, Florida. The tail markings are in Black. (Bill Sides)

...IN THE KNOW WITH PATROL/RECON AIRCRAFT IN ACTION

1087

1092

1062

1068

1086

SR-71 Blackbird
in action
Aircraft No. 55
squadron/signal publications

1055

squadron/signal publications